AI
Driverless Cars
Transmutation

Practical Advances in
Artificial Intelligence and Machine Learning

Dr. Lance B. Eliot, MBA, PhD

Disclaimer: This book is presented solely for educational and entertainment purposes. The author and publisher are not offering it as legal, accounting, or other professional services advice. The author and publisher make no representations or warranties of any kind and assume no liabilities of any kind with respect to the accuracy or completeness of the contents and specifically disclaim any implied warranties of merchantability or fitness of use for a particular purpose. Neither the author nor the publisher shall be held liable or responsible to any person or entity with respect to any loss or incidental or consequential damages caused, or alleged to have been caused, directly or indirectly, by the information or programs contained herein. Every company is different and the advice and strategies contained herein may not be suitable for your situation.

DEDICATION

To my incredible daughter, Lauren, and my incredible son, Michael.
Forest fortuna adiuvat (from the Latin; good fortune favors the brave).

CONTENTS

Lance B. Eliot

ACKNOWLEDGMENTS

I have been the beneficiary of advice and counsel by many friends, colleagues, family, investors, and many others. I want to thank everyone that has aided me throughout my career. I write from the heart and the head, having experienced first-hand what it means to have others around you that support you during the good times and the tough times.

To Warren Bennis, one of my doctoral advisors and ultimately a colleague, I offer my deepest thanks and appreciation, especially for his calm and insightful wisdom and support.

To Mark Stevens and his generous efforts toward funding and supporting the USC Stevens Center for Innovation.

To Lloyd Greif and the USC Lloyd Greif Center for Entrepreneurial Studies for their ongoing encouragement of founders and entrepreneurs.

To Peter Drucker, William Wang, Aaron Levie, Peter Kim, Jon Kraft, Cindy Crawford, Jenny Ming, Steve Milligan, Chis Underwood, Frank Gehry, Buzz Aldrin, Steve Forbes, Bill Thompson, Dave Dillon, Alan Fuerstman, Larry Ellison, Jim Sinegal, John Sperling, Mark Stevenson, Anand Nallathambi, Thomas Barrack, Jr., and many other innovators and leaders that I have met and gained mightily from doing so.

Thanks to Ed Trainor, Kevin Anderson, James Hickey, Wendell Jones, Ken Harris, DuWayne Peterson, Mike Brown, Jim Thornton, Abhi Beniwal, Al Biland, John Nomura, Eliot Weinman, John Desmond, and many others for their unwavering support during my career.

And most of all thanks as always to Lauren and Michael, for their ongoing support and for having seen me writing and heard much of this material during the many months involved in writing it. To their patience and willingness to listen.

Lance B. Eliot

INTRODUCTION

This is a book that provides the newest innovations and the latest Artificial Intelligence (AI) advances about the emerging nature of AI-based autonomous self-driving driverless cars. Via recent advances in Artificial Intelligence (AI) and Machine Learning (ML), we are nearing the day when vehicles can control themselves and will not require and nor rely upon human intervention to perform their driving tasks (or, that <u>allow</u> for human intervention, but only *require* human intervention in very limited ways).

Similar to my other related books, which I describe in a moment and list the chapters in the Appendix A of this book, I am particularly focused on those advances that pertain to self-driving cars. The phrase "autonomous vehicles" is often used to refer to any kind of vehicle, whether it is ground-based or in the air or sea, and whether it is a cargo hauling trailer truck or a conventional passenger car. Though the aspects described in this book are certainly applicable to all kinds of autonomous vehicles, I am focused more so here on cars.

Indeed, I am especially known for my role in aiding the advancement of self-driving cars, serving currently as the Executive Director of the Cybernetic AI Self-Driving Cars Institute. In addition to writing software, designing and developing systems and software for self-driving cars, I also speak and write quite a bit about the topic. This book is a collection of some of my more advanced essays. For those of you that might have seen my essays posted elsewhere, I have updated them and integrated them into this book as one handy cohesive package.

You might be interested in companion books that I have written that provide additional key innovations and fundamentals about self-driving cars. Those books are entitled **"Introduction to Driverless Self-Driving Cars," "Advances in AI and Autonomous Vehicles: Cybernetic Self-Driving Cars," "Self-Driving Cars: "The Mother of All AI Projects," "Innovation and Thought Leadership on Self-Driving Driverless Cars," "New Advances in AI Autonomous Driverless Self-Driving Cars," "Autonomous Vehicle Driverless Self-Driving Cars and Artificial Intelligence," "Transformative Artificial Intelligence**

Driverless Self-Driving Cars," "Disruptive Artificial Intelligence and Driverless Self-Driving Cars, and "State-of-the-Art AI Driverless Self-Driving Cars," and "Top Trends in AI Self-Driving Cars," and "AI Innovations and Self-Driving Cars," "Crucial Advances for AI Driverless Cars," "Sociotechnical Insights and AI Driverless Cars," "Pioneering Advances for AI Driverless Cars" and "Leading Edge Trends for AI Driverless Cars," "The Cutting Edge of AI Autonomous Cars" and "The Next Wave of AI Self-Driving Cars" and "Revolutionary Innovations of AI Self-Driving Cars," and "AI Self-Driving Cars Breakthroughs," "Trailblazing Trends for AI Self-Driving Cars," "Ingenious Strides for AI Driverless Cars," "AI Self-Driving Cars Inventiveness," "Visionary Secrets of AI Driverless Cars," "Spearheading AI Self-Driving Cars," "Spurring AI Self-Driving Cars," "Avant-Garde AI Driverless Cars," "AI Self-Driving Cars Evolvement," "AI Driverless Cars Chrysalis," "Boosting AI Autonomous Cars," "AI Self-Driving Cars Trendsetting," "AI Autonomous Cars Forefront, "AI Autonomous Cars Emergence," "AI Autonomous Cars Progress," "AI Self-Driving Cars Prognosis," "AI Self-Driving Cars Momentum," "AI Self-Driving Cars Headway," "AI Self-Driving Cars Vicissitude," "AI Self-Driving Cars Autonomy," "AI Driverless Cars Transmutation" (they are available on Amazon).

For this book, I am going to borrow my introduction from those companion books, since it does a good job of laying out the landscape of self-driving cars and my overall viewpoints on the topic. The remainder of this book is material that does not appear in the companion books.

INTRODUCTION TO SELF-DRIVING CARS

This is a book about self-driving cars. Someday in the future, we'll all have self-driving cars and this book will perhaps seem antiquated, but right now, we are at the forefront of the self-driving car wave. Daily news bombards us with flashes of new announcements by one car maker or another and leaves the impression that within the next few weeks or maybe months that the self-driving car will be here. A casual non-technical reader would assume from these news flashes that in fact we must be on the cusp of a true self-driving car. We are still quite a distance from having a true self-driving car.

A true self-driving car is akin to a moonshot. In the same manner that getting us to the moon was an incredible feat, likewise, is achieving a true self-driving car. Anybody that suggests or even brashly states that the true self-driving car is nearly here should be viewed with great skepticism. Indeed, you'll see that I often tend to use the word "hogwash" or "crock" when I assess much of the decidedly *fake news* about self-driving cars.

Indeed, I've been writing a popular blog post about self-driving cars and hitting hard on those that try to wave their hands and pretend that we are on the imminent verge of true self-driving cars. For many years, I've been known as the AI Insider. Besides writing about AI, I also develop AI software. I do what I describe. It also gives me insights into what others that are doing AI are really doing versus what it is said they are doing.

Many faithful readers had asked me to pull together my insightful short essays and put them into another book, which you are now holding.

For those of you that have been reading my essays over the years, this collection not only puts them together into one handy package, I also updated the essays and added new material. For those of you that are new to the topic of self-driving cars and AI, I hope you find these essays approachable and informative. I also tend to have a writing style with a bit of a voice, and so you'll see that I am times have a wry sense of humor and poke at conformity.

As a former professor and founder of an AI research lab, I for many years wrote in the formal language of academic writing. I published in referred journals and served as an editor for several AI journals. This writing here is not of the nature, and I have adopted a different and more informal style for these essays. That being said, I also do mention from time-to-time more rigorous material on AI and encourage you all to dig into those deeper and more formal materials if so interested.

I am also an AI practitioner. This means that I write AI software for a living. Currently, I head-up the Cybernetics Self-Driving Car Institute, where we are developing AI software for self-driving cars.

For those of you that are reading this book and have a penchant for writing code, you might consider taking a look at the open source code available for self-driving cars. This is a handy place to start learning how to develop AI for self-driving cars. There are also many new educational courses spring forth. There is a growing body of those wanting to learn about and develop self-driving cars, and a growing body of colleges, labs, and other avenues by which you can learn about self-driving cars.

This book will provide a foundation of aspects that I think will get you ready for those kinds of more advanced training opportunities. If you've already taken those classes, you'll likely find these essays especially interesting as they offer a perspective that I am betting few other instructors or faculty offered to you. These are challenging essays that ask you to think beyond the conventional about self-driving cars.

THE MOTHER OF ALL AI PROJECTS

In June 2017, Apple CEO Tim Cook came out and finally admitted that Apple has been working on a self-driving car. As you'll see in my essays, Apple was enmeshed in secrecy about their self-driving car efforts. We have only been able to read the tea leaves and guess at what Apple has been up to. The notion of an iCar has been floating for quite a while, and self-driving engineers and researchers have been signing tight-lipped Non-Disclosure Agreements (NDA's) to work on projects at Apple that were as shrouded in mystery as any military invasion plans might be.

Tim Cook said something that many others in the Artificial Intelligence (AI) field have been saying, namely, the creation of a self-driving car has got to be the mother of all AI projects. In other words, it is in fact a tremendous moonshot for AI. If a self-driving car can be crafted and the AI works as we hope, it means that we have made incredible strides with AI and that therefore it opens many other worlds of potential breakthrough accomplishments that AI can solve.

Is this hyperbole? Am I just trying to make AI seem like a miracle worker and so provide self-aggrandizing statements for those of us writing the AI software for self-driving cars? No, it is not hyperbole. Developing a true self-driving car is really, really, really hard to do. Let me take a moment to explain why. As a side note, I realize that the Apple CEO is known for at times uttering hyperbole, and he had previously said for example that the year 2012 was "the mother of all years," and he had said that the release of iOS 10 was "the mother of all releases" – all of which does suggest he likes to use the handy "mother of" expression. But, I assure you, in terms of true self-driving cars, he has hit the nail on the head. For sure.

When you think about a moonshot and how we got to the moon, there are some identifiable characteristics and those same aspects can be applied to creating a true self-driving car. You'll notice that I keep putting the word "true" in front of the self-driving car expression. I do so because as per my essay about the various levels of self-driving cars, there are some self-driving cars that are only somewhat of a self-driving car. The somewhat versions are ones that require a human driver to be ready to intervene. In my view, that's not a true self-driving car. A true self-driving car is one that requires no human driver intervention at all. It is a car that can entirely undertake via automation the driving task without any human driver needed. This is the essence of what is known as a Level 5 self-driving car. We are currently at the Level 2 and Level 3 mark, and not yet at Level 5.

Getting to the moon involved aspects such as having big stretch goals, incremental progress, experimentation, innovation, and so on. Let's review how this applied to the moonshot of the bygone era, and how it applies to the self-driving car moonshot of today.

Big Stretch Goal

Trying to take a human and deliver the human to the moon, and bring them back, safely, was an extremely large stretch goal at the time. No one knew whether it could be done. The technology wasn't available yet. The cost was huge. The determination would need to be fierce. Etc. To reach a Level 5 self-driving car is going to be the same. It is a big stretch goal. We can readily get to the Level 3, and we are able to see the Level 4 just up ahead, but a Level 5 is still an unknown as to if it is doable. It should eventually be doable and in the same way that we thought we'd eventually get to the moon, but when it will occur is a different story.

Incremental Progress

Getting to the moon did not happen overnight in one fell swoop. It took years and years of incremental progress to get there. Likewise for self-driving cars. Google has famously been striving to get to the Level 5, and pretty much been willing to forgo dealing with the intervening levels, but most of the other self-driving car makers are doing the incremental route. Let's get a good Level 2 and a somewhat Level 3 going. Then, let's improve the Level 3 and get a somewhat Level 4 going. Then, let's improve the Level 4 and finally arrive at a Level 5. This seems to be the prevalent way that we are going to achieve the true self-driving car.

Experimentation

You likely know that there were various experiments involved in perfecting the approach and technology to get to the moon. As per making incremental progress, we first tried to see if we could get a rocket to go into space and safety return, then put a monkey in there, then with a human, then we went all the way to the moon but didn't land, and finally we arrived at the mission that actually landed on the moon. Self-driving cars are the same way. We are doing simulations of self-driving cars. We do testing of self-driving cars on private land under controlled situations. We do testing of self-driving cars on public roadways, often having to meet regulatory requirements including for example having an engineer or equivalent in the car to take over the controls if needed. And so on. Experiments big and small are needed to figure out what works and what doesn't.

Innovation

There are already some advances in AI that are allowing us to progress toward self-driving cars. We are going to need even more advances. Innovation in all aspects of technology are going to be required to achieve a true self-driving car. By no means do we already have everything in-hand that we need to get there. Expect new inventions and new approaches, new algorithms, etc.

Setbacks

Most of the pundits are avoiding talking about potential setbacks in the progress toward self-driving cars. Getting to the moon involved many setbacks, some of which you never have heard of and were buried at the time so as to not dampen enthusiasm and funding for getting to the moon. A recurring theme in many of my included essays is that there are going to be setbacks as we try to arrive at a true self-driving car. Take a deep breath and be ready. I just hope the setbacks don't completely stop progress. I am sure that it will cause progress to alter in a manner that we've not yet seen in the self-driving car field. I liken the self-driving car of today to the excitement everyone had for Uber when it first got going. Today, we have a different view of Uber and with each passing day there are more regulations to the ride sharing business and more concerns raised. The darling child only stays a darling until finally that child acts up. It will happen the same with self-driving cars.

SELF-DRIVING CARS CHALLENGES

But what exactly makes things so hard to have a true self-driving car, you might be asking. You have seen cruise control for years and years. You've lately seen cars that can do parallel parking. You've seen YouTube videos of Tesla drivers that put their hands out the window as their car zooms along the highway, and seen to therefore be in a self-driving car. Aren't we just needing to put a few more sensors onto a car and then we'll have in-hand a true self-driving car? Nope.

Consider for a moment the nature of the driving task. We don't just let anyone at any age drive a car. Worldwide, most countries won't license a driver until the age of 18, though many do allow a learner's permit at the age of 15 or 16. Some suggest that a younger age would be physically too small to reach the controls of the car. Though this might be the case, we could easily adjust the controls to allow for younger aged and thus smaller stature.

It's not their physical size that matters. It's their cognitive development that matters.

To drive a car, you need to be able to reason about the car, what the car can and cannot do. You need to know how to operate the car. You need to know about how other cars on the road drive. You need to know what is allowed in driving such as speed limits and driving within marked lanes. You need to be able to react to situations and be able to avoid getting into accidents. You need to ascertain when to hit your brakes, when to steer clear of a pedestrian, and how to keep from ramming that motorcyclist that just cut you off.

Many of us had taken courses on driving. We studied about driving and took driver training. We had to take a test and pass it to be able to drive. The point being that though most adults take the driving task for granted, and we often "mindlessly" drive our cars, there is a significant amount of cognitive effort that goes into driving a car. After a while, it becomes second nature. You don't especially think about how you drive, you just do it. But, if you watch a novice driver, say a teenager learning to drive, you suddenly realize that there is a lot more complexity to it than we seem to realize.

Furthermore, driving is a very serious task. I recall when my daughter and son first learned to drive. They are both very conscientious people. They wanted to make sure that whatever they did, they did well, and that they did not harm anyone. Every day, when you get into a car, it is probably around 4,000 pounds of hefty metal and plastics (about two tons), and it is a lethal weapon. Think about it. You drive down the street in an object that weighs two tons and with the engine it can accelerate and ram into anything you want to hit. The damage a car can inflict is very scary. Both my children were surprised that they were being given the right to maneuver this monster of a beast that could cause tremendous harm entirely by merely letting go of the steering wheel for a moment or taking your eyes off the road.

In fact, in the United States alone there are about 30,000 deaths per year by auto accidents, which is around 100 per day. Given that there are about 263 million cars in the United States, I am actually more amazed that the number of fatalities is not a lot higher. During my morning commute, I look at all the thousands of cars on the freeway around me, and I think that if all of them decided to go zombie and drive in a crazy maniac way, there would be many people dead. Somehow, incredibly, each day, most people drive relatively safely. To me, that's a miracle right there. Getting millions and millions of people to be safe and sane when behind the wheel of a two ton mobile object, it's a feat that we as a society should admire with pride.

So, hopefully you are in agreement that the driving task requires a great deal of cognition. You don't' need to be especially smart to drive a car, and we've done quite a bit to make car driving viable for even the average dolt. There isn't an IQ test that you need to take to drive a car. If you can read and write, and pass a test, you pretty much can legally drive a car. There are of course some that drive a car and are not legally permitted to do so, plus there are private areas such as farms where drivers are young, but for public roadways in the United States, you can be generally of average intelligence (or less) and be able to legally drive.

This though makes it seem like the cognitive effort must not be much. If the cognitive effort was truly hard, wouldn't we only have Einstein's that could drive a car? We have made sure to keep the driving task as simple as we can, by making the controls easy and relatively standardized, and by having roads that are relatively standardized, and so on. It is as though Disneyland has put their Autopia into the real-world, by us all as a society agreeing that roads will be a certain way, and we'll all abide by the various rules of driving.

A modest cognitive task by a human is still something that stymies AI. You certainly know that AI has been able to beat chess players and be good at other kinds of games. This type of narrow cognition is not what car driving is about. Car driving is much wider. It requires knowledge about the world, which a chess playing AI system does not need to know. The cognitive aspects of driving are on the one hand seemingly simple, but at the same time require layer upon layer of knowledge about cars, people, roads, rules, and a myriad of other "common sense" aspects. We don't have any AI systems today that have that same kind of breadth and depth of awareness and knowledge.

As revealed in my essays, the self-driving car of today is using trickery to do particular tasks. It is all very narrow in operation. Plus, it currently assumes that a human driver is ready to intervene. It is like a child that we have taught to stack blocks, but we are needed to be right there in case the child stacks them too high and they begin to fall over. AI of today is brittle, it is narrow, and it does not approach the cognitive abilities of humans. This is why the true self-driving car is somewhere out in the future.

Another aspect to the driving task is that it is not solely a mind exercise. You do need to use your senses to drive. You use your eyes a vision sensors to see the road ahead. You vision capability is like a streaming video, which your brain needs to continually analyze as you drive. Where is the road? Is there a pedestrian in the way? Is there another car ahead of you? Your senses are relying a flood of info to your brain. Self-driving cars are trying to do the same, by using cameras, radar, ultrasound, and lasers. This is an attempt at mimicking how humans have senses and sensory apparatus.

Thus, the driving task is mental and physical. You use your senses, you use your arms and legs to manipulate the controls of the car, and you use your brain to assess the sensory info and direct your limbs to act upon the controls of the car. This all happens instantly. If you've ever perhaps gotten something in your eye and only had one eye available to drive with, you suddenly realize how dependent upon vision you are. If you have a broken foot with a cast, you suddenly realize how hard it is to control the brake pedal and the accelerator. If you've taken medication and your brain is maybe sluggish, you suddenly realize how much mental strain is required to drive a car.

An AI system that plays chess only needs to be focused on playing chess. The physical aspects aren't important because usually a human moves the chess pieces or the chessboard is shown on an electronic display. Using AI for a more life-and-death task such as analyzing MRI images of patients, this again does not require physical capabilities and instead is done by examining images of bits.

Driving a car is a true life-and-death task. It is a use of AI that can easily and at any moment produce death. For those colleagues of mine that are developing this AI, as am I, we need to keep in mind the somber aspects of this. We are producing software that will have in its virtual hands the lives of the occupants of the car, and the lives of those in other nearby cars, and the lives of nearby pedestrians, etc. Chess is not usually a life-or-death matter.

Driving is all around us. Cars are everywhere. Most of today's AI applications involve only a small number of people. Or, they are behind the scenes and we as humans have other recourse if the AI messes up. AI that is driving a car at 80 miles per hour on a highway had better not mess up. The consequences are grave. Multiply this by the number of cars, if we could put magically self-driving into every car in the USA, we'd have AI running in the 263 million cars. That's a lot of AI spread around. This is AI on a massive scale that we are not doing today and that offers both promise and potential peril.

There are some that want AI for self-driving cars because they envision a world without any car accidents. They envision a world in which there is no car congestion and all cars cooperate with each other. These are wonderful utopian visions.

They are also very misleading. The adoption of self-driving cars is going to be incremental and not overnight. We cannot economically just junk all existing cars. Nor are we going to be able to affordably retrofit existing cars. It is more likely that self-driving cars will be built into new cars and that over many years of gradual replacement of existing cars that we'll see the mix of self-driving cars become substantial in the real-world.

In these essays, I have tried to offer technological insights without being overly technical in my description, and also blended the business, societal, and economic aspects too. Technologists need to consider the non-technological impacts of what they do. Non-technologists should be aware of what is being developed.

We all need to work together to collectively be prepared for the enormous disruption and transformative aspects of true self-driving cars. We all need to be involved in this mother of all AI projects.

WHAT THIS BOOK PROVIDES

What does this book provide to you? It introduces many of the key elements about self-driving cars and does so with an AI based perspective. I weave together technical and non-technical aspects, readily going from being concerned about the cognitive capabilities of the driving task and how the technology is embodying this into self-driving cars, and in the next breath I discuss the societal and economic aspects.

They are all intertwined because that's the way reality is. You cannot separate out the technology per se, and instead must consider it within the milieu of what is being invented and innovated, and do so with a mindset towards the contemporary mores and culture that shape what we are doing and what we hope to do.

WHY THIS BOOK

I wrote this book to try and bring to the public view many aspects about self-driving cars that nobody seems to be discussing.

For business leaders that are either involved in making self-driving cars or that are going to leverage self-driving cars, I hope that this book will enlighten you as to the risks involved and ways in which you should be strategizing about how to deal with those risks.

For entrepreneurs, startups and other businesses that want to enter into the self-driving car market that is emerging, I hope this book sparks your interest in doing so, and provides some sense of what might be prudent to pursue.

For researchers that study self-driving cars, I hope this book spurs your interest in the risks and safety issues of self-driving cars, and also nudges you toward conducting research on those aspects.

For students in computer science or related disciplines, I hope this book will provide you with interesting and new ideas and material, for which you might conduct research or provide some career direction insights for you.

For AI companies and high-tech companies pursuing self-driving cars, this book will hopefully broaden your view beyond just the mere coding and development needed to make self-driving cars.

For all readers, I hope that you will find the material in this book to be stimulating. Some of it will be repetitive of things you already know. But I am pretty sure that you'll also find various eureka moments whereby you'll discover a new technique or approach that you had not earlier thought of. I am also betting that there will be material that forces you to rethink some of your current practices.

I am not saying you will suddenly have an epiphany and change what you are doing. I do think though that you will reconsider or perhaps revisit what you are doing.

For anyone choosing to use this book for teaching purposes, please take a look at my suggestions for doing so, as described in the Appendix. I have found the material handy in courses that I have taught, and likewise other faculty have told me that they have found the material handy, in some cases as extended readings and in other instances as a core part of their course (depending on the nature of the class).

In my writing for this book, I have tried carefully to blend both the practitioner and the academic styles of writing. It is not as dense as is typical academic journal writing, but at the same time offers depth by going into the nuances and trade-offs of various practices.

The word "deep" is in vogue today, meaning getting deeply into a subject or topic, and so is the word "unpack" which means to tease out the underlying aspects of a subject or topic. I have sought to offer material that addresses an issue or topic by going relatively deeply into it and make sure that it is well unpacked.

In any book about AI, it is difficult to use our everyday words without having some of them be misinterpreted. Specifically, it is easy to anthropomorphize AI. When I say that an AI system "knows" something, I do not want you to construe that the AI system has sentience and "knows" in the same way that humans do. They aren't that way, as yet. I have tried to use quotes around such words from time-to-time to emphasize that the words I am using should not be misinterpreted to ascribe true human intelligence to the AI systems that we know of today. If I used quotes around all such words, the book would be very difficult to read, and so I am doing so judiciously. Please keep that in mind as you read the material, thanks.

Some of the material is time-based in terms of covering underway activities, and though some of it might decay, nonetheless I believe you'll find the material useful and informative.

COMPANION BOOKS

1. **"Introduction to Driverless Self-Driving Cars"** by Dr. Lance Eliot
2. **"Innovation and Thought Leadership on Self-Driving Driverless Cars"** by Dr. Lance Eliot
3. **"Advances in AI and Autonomous Vehicles: Cybernetic Self-Driving Cars"** by Dr. Lance Eliot
4. **"Self-Driving Cars: The Mother of All AI Projects"** by Dr. Lance Eliot
5. **"New Advances in AI Autonomous Driverless Self-Driving Cars"** by Dr. Lance Eliot
6. **"Autonomous Vehicle Driverless Self-Driving Cars and Artificial Intelligence"** by Dr. Lance Eliot and Michael B. Eliot
7. **"Transformative Artificial Intelligence Driverless Self-Driving Cars"** by Dr. Lance Eliot
8. **"Disruptive Artificial Intelligence and Driverless Self-Driving Cars"** by Dr. Lance Eliot
9. **"State-of-the-Art AI Driverless Self-Driving Cars"** by Dr. Lance Eliot
10. **"Top Trends in AI Self-Driving Cars"** by Dr. Lance Eliot
11. **"AI Innovations and Self-Driving Cars"** by Dr. Lance Eliot
12. **"Crucial Advances for AI Driverless Cars"** by Dr. Lance Eliot
13. **"Sociotechnical Insights and AI Driverless Cars"** by Dr. Lance Eliot.
14. **"Pioneering Advances for AI Driverless Cars"** by Dr. Lance Eliot
15. **"Leading Edge Trends for AI Driverless Cars"** by Dr. Lance Eliot
16. **"The Cutting Edge of AI Autonomous Cars"** by Dr. Lance Eliot
17. **"The Next Wave of AI Self-Driving Cars"** by Dr. Lance Eliot
18. **"Revolutionary Innovations of AI Driverless Cars"** by Dr. Lance Eliot
19. **"AI Self-Driving Cars Breakthroughs"** by Dr. Lance Eliot
20. **"Trailblazing Trends for AI Self-Driving Cars"** by Dr. Lance Eliot
21. **"Ingenious Strides for AI Driverless Cars"** by Dr. Lance Eliot
22. **"AI Self-Driving Cars Inventiveness"** by Dr. Lance Eliot
23. **"Visionary Secrets of AI Driverless Cars"** by Dr. Lance Eliot
24. **"Spearheading AI Self-Driving Cars"** by Dr. Lance Eliot
25. **"Spurring AI Self-Driving Cars"** by Dr. Lance Eliot
26. **"Avant-Garde AI Driverless Cars"** by Dr. Lance Eliot
27. **"AI Self-Driving Cars Evolvement"** by Dr. Lance Eliot
28. **"AI Driverless Cars Chrysalis"** by Dr. Lance Eliot
29. **"Boosting AI Autonomous Cars"** by Dr. Lance Eliot
30. **"AI Self-Driving Cars Trendsetting"** by Dr. Lance Eliot
31. **"AI Autonomous Cars Forefront"** by Dr. Lance Eliot
32. **"AI Autonomous Cars Emergence"** by Dr. Lance Eliot
33. **"AI Autonomous Cars Progress"** by Dr. Lance Eliot
34. **"AI Self-Driving Cars Prognosis"** by Dr. Lance Eliot
35. **"AI Self-Driving Cars Momentum"** by Dr. Lance Eliot
36. **"AI Self-Driving Cars Headway"** by Dr. Lance Eliot
37. **"AI Self-Driving Cars Vicissitude"** by Dr. Lance Eliot
38. **"AI Self-Driving Cars Autonomy"** by Dr. Lance Eliot
39. **"AI Driverless Cars Transmutation"** by Dr. Lance Eliot

These books are available on Amazon and at other major global booksellers.

CHAPTER 1

ELIOT FRAMEWORK FOR AI SELF-DRIVING CARS

CHAPTER 1

ELIOT FRAMEWORK FOR
AI SELF-DRIVING CARS

This chapter is a core foundational aspect for understanding AI self-driving cars and I have used this same chapter in several of my other books to introduce the reader to essential elements of this field. Once you've read this chapter, you'll be prepared to read the rest of the material since the foundational essence of the components of autonomous AI driverless self-driving cars will have been established for you.

When I give presentations about self-driving cars and teach classes on the topic, I have found it helpful to provide a framework around which the various key elements of self-driving cars can be understood and organized (see diagram at the end of this chapter). The framework needs to be simple enough to convey the overarching elements, but at the same time not so simple that it belies the true complexity of self-driving cars. As such, I am going to describe the framework here and try to offer in a thousand words (or more!) what the framework diagram itself intends to portray.

The core elements on the diagram are numbered for ease of reference. The numbering does not suggest any kind of prioritization of the elements. Each element is crucial. Each element has a purpose, and otherwise would not be included in the framework. For some self-driving cars, a particular element might be more important or somehow distinguished in comparison to other self-driving cars.

You could even use the framework to rate a particular self-driving car, doing so by gauging how well it performs in each of the elements of the framework. I will describe each of the elements, one at a time. After doing so, I'll discuss aspects that illustrate how the elements interact and perform during the overall effort of a self-driving car.

At the Cybernetic Self-Driving Car Institute, we use the framework to keep track of what we are working on, and how we are developing software that fills in what is needed to achieve Level 5 self-driving cars.

D-01: Sensor Capture

Let's start with the one element that often gets the most attention in the press about self-driving cars, namely, the sensory devices for a self-driving car.

On the framework, the box labeled as D-01 indicates "Sensor Capture" and refers to the processes of the self-driving car that involve collecting data from the myriad of sensors that are used for a self-driving car. The types of devices typically involved are listed, such as the use of mono cameras, stereo cameras, LIDAR devices, radar systems, ultrasonic devices, GPS, IMU, and so on.

These devices are tasked with obtaining data about the status of the self-driving car and the world around it. Some of the devices are continually providing updates, while others of the devices await an indication by the self-driving car that the device is supposed to collect data. The data might be first transformed in some fashion by the device itself, or it might instead be fed directly into the sensor capture as raw data. At that point, it might be up to the sensor capture processes to do transformations on the data. This all varies depending upon the nature of the devices being used and how the devices were designed and developed.

D-02: Sensor Fusion

Imagine that your eyeballs receive visual images, your nose receives odors, your ears receive sounds, and in essence each of your distinct sensory devices is getting some form of input. The input befits the nature of the device. Likewise, for a self-driving car, the cameras provide visual images, the radar returns radar reflections, and so on.

Each device provides the data as befits what the device does.

At some point, using the analogy to humans, you need to merge together what your eyes see, what your nose smells, what your ears hear, and piece it all together into a larger sense of what the world is all about and what is happening around you. Sensor fusion is the action of taking the singular aspects from each of the devices and putting them together into a larger puzzle.

Sensor fusion is a tough task. There are some devices that might not be working at the time of the sensor capture. Or, there might some devices that are unable to report well what they have detected. Again, using a human analogy, suppose you are in a dark room and so your eyes cannot see much. At that point, you might need to rely more so on your ears and what you hear. The same is true for a self-driving car. If the cameras are obscured due to snow and sleet, it might be that the radar can provide a greater indication of what the external conditions consist of.

In the case of a self-driving car, there can be a plethora of such sensory devices. Each is reporting what it can. Each might have its difficulties. Each might have its limitations, such as how far ahead it can detect an object. All of these limitations need to be considered during the sensor fusion task.

D-03: Virtual World Model

For humans, we presumably keep in our minds a model of the world around us when we are driving a car. In your mind, you know that the car is going at say 60 miles per hour and that you are on a freeway. You have a model in your mind that your car is surrounded by other cars, and that there are lanes to the freeway. Your model is not only based on what you can see, hear, etc., but also what you know about the nature of the world. You know that at any moment that car ahead of you can smash on its brakes, or the car behind you can ram into your car, or that the truck in the next lane might swerve into your lane.

The AI of the self-driving car needs to have a virtual world model, which it then keeps updated with whatever it is receiving from the sensor fusion, which received its input from the sensor capture and the sensory devices.

D-04: System Action Plan

By having a virtual world model, the AI of the self-driving car is able to keep track of where the car is and what is happening around the car. In addition, the AI needs to determine what to do next. Should the self-driving car hit its brakes? Should the self-driving car stay in its lane or swerve into the lane to the left? Should the self-driving car accelerate or slow down?

A system action plan needs to be prepared by the AI of the self-driving car. The action plan specifies what actions should be taken. The actions need to pertain to the status of the virtual world model. Plus, the actions need to be realizable.

This realizability means that the AI cannot just assert that the self-driving car should suddenly sprout wings and fly. Instead, the AI must be bound by whatever the self-driving car can actually do, such as coming to a halt in a distance of X feet at a speed of Y miles per hour, rather than perhaps asserting that the self-driving car come to a halt in 0 feet as though it could instantaneously come to a stop while it is in motion.

D-05: Controls Activation

The system action plan is implemented by activating the controls of the car to act according to what the plan stipulates. This might mean that the accelerator control is commanded to increase the speed of the car. Or, the steering control is commanded to turn the steering wheel 30 degrees to the left or right.

One question arises as to whether or not the controls respond as they are commanded to do. In other words, suppose the AI has commanded the accelerator to increase, but for some reason it does not do so. Or, maybe it tries to do so, but the speed of the car does not increase. The controls activation feeds back into the virtual world model, and simultaneously the virtual world model is getting updated from the sensors, the sensor capture, and the sensor fusion. This allows the AI to ascertain what has taken place as a result of the controls being commanded to take some kind of action.

By the way, please keep in mind that though the diagram seems to have a linear progression to it, the reality is that these are all aspects of the self-driving car that are happening in parallel and simultaneously. The sensors are capturing data, meanwhile the sensor fusion is taking place, meanwhile the virtual model is being updated, meanwhile the system action plan is being formulated and reformulated, meanwhile the controls are being activated.

This is the same as a human being that is driving a car. They are eyeballing the road, meanwhile they are fusing in their mind the sights, sounds, etc., meanwhile their mind is updating their model of the world around them, meanwhile they are formulating an action plan of what to do, and meanwhile they are pushing their foot onto the pedals and steering the car. In the normal course of driving a car, you are doing all of these at once. I mention this so that when you look at the diagram, you will think of the boxes as processes that are all happening at the same time, and not as though only one happens and then the next.

They are shown diagrammatically in a simplistic manner to help comprehend what is taking place. You though should also realize that they are working in parallel and simultaneous with each other. This is a tough aspect in that the inter-element communications involve latency and other aspects that must be taken into account. There can be delays in one element updating and then sharing its latest status with other elements.

D-06: Automobile & CAN

Contemporary cars use various automotive electronics and a Controller Area Network (CAN) to serve as the components that underlie the driving aspects of a car. There are Electronic Control Units (ECU's) which control subsystems of the car, such as the engine, the brakes, the doors, the windows, and so on.

The elements D-01, D-02, D-03, D-04, D-05 are layered on top of the D-06, and must be aware of the nature of what the D-06 is able to do and not do.

D-07: In-Car Commands

Humans are going to be occupants in self-driving cars. In a Level 5 self-driving car, there must be some form of communication that takes place between the humans and the self-driving car. For example, I go into a self-driving car and tell it that I want to be driven over to Disneyland, and along the way I want to stop at In-and-Out Burger. The self-driving car now parses what I've said and tries to then establish a means to carry out my wishes.

In-car commands can happen at any time during a driving journey. Though my example was about an in-car command when I first got into my self-driving car, it could be that while the self-driving car is carrying out the journey that I change my mind. Perhaps after getting stuck in traffic, I tell the self-driving car to forget about getting the burgers and just head straight over to the theme park. The self-driving car needs to be alert to in-car commands throughout the journey.

D-08: V2X Communications

We will ultimately have self-driving cars communicating with each other, doing so via V2V (Vehicle-to-Vehicle) communications. We will also have self-driving cars that communicate with the roadways and other aspects of the transportation infrastructure, doing so via V2I (Vehicle-to-Infrastructure).

The variety of ways in which a self-driving car will be communicating with other cars and infrastructure is being called V2X, whereby the letter X means whatever else we identify as something that a car should or would want to communicate with. The V2X communications will be taking place simultaneous with everything else on the diagram, and those other elements will need to incorporate whatever it gleans from those V2X communications.

D-09: Deep Learning

The use of Deep Learning permeates all other aspects of the self-driving car. The AI of the self-driving car will be using deep learning to do a better job at the systems action plan, and at the controls activation, and at the sensor fusion, and so on.

Currently, the use of artificial neural networks is the most prevalent form of deep learning. Based on large swaths of data, the neural networks attempt to "learn" from the data and therefore direct the efforts of the self-driving car accordingly.

D-10: Tactical AI

Tactical AI is the element of dealing with the moment-to-moment driving of the self-driving car. Is the self-driving car staying in its lane of the freeway? Is the car responding appropriately to the controls commands? Are the sensory devices working?

For human drivers, the tactical equivalent can be seen when you watch a novice driver such as a teenager that is first driving. They are focused on the mechanics of the driving task, keeping their eye on the road while also trying to properly control the car.

D-11: Strategic AI

The Strategic AI aspects of a self-driving car are dealing with the larger picture of what the self-driving car is trying to do. If I had asked that the self-driving car take me to Disneyland, there is an overall journey map that needs to be kept and maintained.

There is an interaction between the Strategic AI and the Tactical AI. The Strategic AI is wanting to keep on the mission of the driving, while the Tactical AI is focused on the particulars underway in the driving effort. If the Tactical AI seems to wander away from the overarching mission, the Strategic AI wants to see why and get things back on track. If the Tactical AI realizes that there is something amiss on the self-driving car, it needs to alert the Strategic AI accordingly and have an adjustment to the overarching mission that is underway.

D-12: Self-Aware AI

Very few of the self-driving cars being developed are including a Self-Aware AI element, which we at the Cybernetic Self-Driving Car Institute believe is crucial to Level 5 self-driving cars.

The Self-Aware AI element is intended to watch over itself, in the sense that the AI is making sure that the AI is working as intended. Suppose you had a human driving a car, and they were starting to drive erratically. Hopefully, their own self-awareness would make them realize they themselves are driving poorly, such as perhaps starting to fall asleep after having been driving for hours on end. If you had a passenger in the car, they might be able to alert the driver if the driver is starting to do something amiss. This is exactly what the Self-Aware

AI element tries to do, it becomes the overseer of the AI, and tries to detect when the AI has become faulty or confused, and then find ways to overcome the issue.

D-13: Economic

The economic aspects of a self-driving car are not per se a technology aspect of a self-driving car, but the economics do indeed impact the nature of a self-driving car. For example, the cost of outfitting a self-driving car with every kind of possible sensory device is prohibitive, and so choices need to be made about which devices are used. And, for those sensory devices chosen, whether they would have a full set of features or a more limited set of features.

We are going to have self-driving cars that are at the low-end of a consumer cost point, and others at the high-end of a consumer cost point. You cannot expect that the self-driving car at the low-end is going to be as robust as the one at the high-end. I realize that many of the self-driving car pundits are acting as though all self-driving cars will be the same, but they won't be. Just like anything else, we are going to have self-driving cars that have a range of capabilities. Some will be better than others. Some will be safer than others. This is the way of the real-world, and so we need to be thinking about the economics aspects when considering the nature of self-driving cars.

D-14: Societal

This component encompasses the societal aspects of AI which also impacts the technology of self-driving cars. For example, the famous Trolley Problem involves what choices should a self-driving car make when faced with life-and-death matters. If the self-driving car is about to either hit a child standing in the roadway, or instead ram into a tree at the side of the road and possibly kill the humans in the self-driving car, which choice should be made?

We need to keep in mind the societal aspects will underlie the AI of the self-driving car. Whether we are aware of it explicitly or not, the AI will have embedded into it various societal assumptions.

D-15: Innovation

I included the notion of innovation into the framework because we can anticipate that whatever a self-driving car consists of, it will continue to be innovated over time. The self-driving cars coming out in the next several years will undoubtedly be different and less innovative than the versions that come out in ten years hence, and so on.

Framework Overall

For those of you that want to learn about self-driving cars, you can potentially pick a particular element and become specialized in that aspect. Some engineers are focusing on the sensory devices. Some engineers focus on the controls activation. And so on. There are specialties in each of the elements.

Researchers are likewise specializing in various aspects. For example, there are researchers that are using Deep Learning to see how best it can be used for sensor fusion. There are other researchers that are using Deep Learning to derive good System Action Plans. Some are studying how to develop AI for the Strategic aspects of the driving task, while others are focused on the Tactical aspects.

A well-prepared all-around software developer that is involved in self-driving cars should be familiar with all of the elements, at least to the degree that they know what each element does. This is important since whatever piece of the pie that the software developer works on, they need to be knowledgeable about what the other elements are doing.

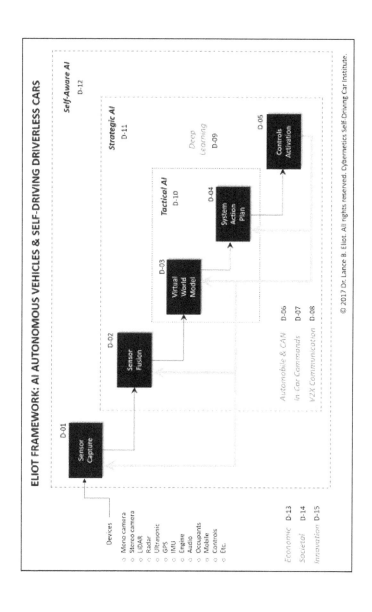

ELIOT FRAMEWORK: AI AUTONOMOUS VEHICLES & SELF-DRIVING DRIVERLESS CARS

Lance B. Eliot

CHAPTER 2
BACKUP DRIVERS
AND
AI SELF-DRIVING CARS

CHAPTER 2

BACKUP DRIVERS
AND AI SELF-DRIVING CARS

When you get behind the wheel of a car, it is a solemn duty and one that holds you responsible for what the car ends up doing.

While driving, if you suddenly realize that you are about to ram into another car, the odds are that your cognitive focus on the driving task will aid you toward quickly maneuvering to avoid the potential crash. Your mind will command your arms to steer away from the other car and your legs might be mentally instructed to slam on the brakes.

At times, you can become distracted from the driving task such as trying to look at the latest text message on your cell phone or while grabbing that eggnog latte that you purchased earlier in the morning.

Being distracted means that you can lose precious time when having to make split-second decisions about the driving task.

Adverse outcomes due to being mentally adrift of the driving task can be horrid and lead to deaths and injuries. Indeed, in the United States alone, there are about 40,000 annual car-related deaths and over 1.2 million injuries as a result of car crashes, many of which are caused by drivers that weren't fully attentive to the driving chore.

There is time involved in what's called the driving task cycle, consisting of your having to think about a driving situation, mentally craft a plan of action, instinctively convey the plan to your limbs, and then have your limbs enact the plan, notably all part of a delicate dance that keeps you and your car from getting into trouble.

For most of us, we are in a heightened state of readiness while driving a car and the driving task cycle is running over-and-over in our minds as we command the car on the roadway.

Your eyes are on the road, your hands are on the steering wheel, your feet are on the pedals of the car, and your mind is closely watching the world around the car as you scan for what's ahead of you.

It's like being a cat that's ready to pounce.

Imagine though if you were somewhat a second fiddle when it came to the act of driving a car and being behind the wheel.

You might recall that teenage novice drivers often learned how to drive a car by sitting in the driver's seat and meanwhile an instructor sat in the passenger's seat and had a second set of driving controls.

The newbie driver was the active driver and the instructor was essentially a passive driver. If the teenager began to go astray, the instructor could first try to tell the novice to correct whatever is going wrong, and then when things went especially awry the instructor might take over the driving controls to steer out of harm's way.

Suppose you were that second driver, the one that's not actually actively driving the car, and yet you are presumably there to immediately step into the driving effort as needed.

It's a tough spot to be in.

On the one hand, you might be greatly tempted to use your driving controls at the slightest indication that the novice driver is having issues.

Does the teenage driver see those pedestrians at the crosswalk, well, maybe it is safest for you to take over the driving controls just in case?

Or, it seems like the car is going too fast, best to tap your foot on the brakes, rather than trying to explain to the novice driver that the car needs to slow down.

And so on.

Unfortunately, each time that you act, you are undermining the newbie driver and not allowing them to fully command the car. Your job is intended to allow the teenager to figure out how to drive and mainly ensure that dire situations are averted.

There is an awkwardness in co-sharing the driving task, and the second driver is like a cat that's not quite supposed to pounce, but still seem ready to pounce, yet only should pounce when truly needed. Unless you are a soothsayer that can see the future, it is hard to know when you ought to intervene and when there's no need to intervene.

Furthermore, if you provide a lot of latitude to the newbie driver, the odds are that you will delay in intervening when the crucial moment arises, meaning that it might be too late by the time you do make use of the driving controls.

Life is sometimes like being between a rock and a hard place.

You've just been introduced to a vital role for today's self-driving cars that are being tested on our public roadways, namely the role of assigned human drivers that serve as the backup to an AI system that's driving a self-driving car.

Human Backup Drivers For AI Self-Driving Cars

These backup drivers are often referred to as test drivers, though in the case of their being in a second fiddle capacity, they are more aptly called fallback test drivers.

A test driver would be someone that is the primary driver of a car, doing so to test out how the car maneuvers and works.

A fallback test driver is a person that is akin to the second driver in my example of a teenager learning to drive. They don't actively drive the car per se and instead allow the AI to do so, meanwhile they are supposed to be ready to take over the driving controls when needed.

The in-vehicle fallback test driver (IFTD) serves as a last line of defense, aiming to keep an eye on what the AI driving system is doing, and then intervene when needed, but only when needed and not jumping the gun in doing so.

Sometimes people think that being a fallback test driver is a cushy job and easy as pie.

You sit in a nifty state-of-the-art equipped car and do nothing for say 99% of the time. Yes, that might be true, though think about the 99% of the time and the 1% of the time.

During the 99% of the time, you are theoretically at the ready, all the time, perhaps for hours on end as the driverless car goes throughout a city and town doing its driving learning and testing.

I assure you that boredom can become a significant problem.

Sure, you are presumably on the edge of your seat, but can you really remain in that state for hours at a stretch, doing nothing other than waiting to ascertain whether you should intervene?

And, consider the 1% of the time when you do take over the controls.

The chances are that you took over the controls because something untoward was about to happen.

Plus, later, you might be required to explain why you intervened. If you intervened and there wasn't any notable reason to do so, you are likely seen as a jackrabbit that isn't letting the AI do its thing. It is hard to prove that your efforts avoided a car accident, since there wasn't a car accident that happened, and it could be that no such accident would have occurred anyway, such that the AI might not have gotten into an accident at all.

In your mind, you might repeatedly be saying this to yourself: Should I intervene now or should I not?

The most insidious phenomenon is when a driverless car seems to be performing ably for hours on end, and you can become complacent and begin to let your guard down. You assume that the self-driving car is always going to do the right thing.

So, add together being lulled into complacency, along with the boredom from doing "nothing" (though you are indeed supposed to be doing something, you are tasked with watching the road and acting to ensure the safety of the car driving), and you have a potent combination that can dramatically undercut the purpose of having a fallback test driver.

Worst Practices Have Been Occurring

Worst practices have been aplenty by some of the firms that initially opted to put their self-driving cars on our roadways.

A firm might falsely think that the fallback test driver is an insignificant role and therefore hire just about anyone to do the job. If you are breathing and can drive a car, you are hired.

A firm might pay peanuts to the fallback test drivers, figuring it really is a minimum wage job. Keep in mind that flipping burgers versus being inside a multi-ton vehicle that can ram and kill people are two different things.

Low pay might also tend toward having fallback test drivers that take the position as a second job and show-up to be the co-sharing driver after having worked a full day in say a nearby manufacturing plant. Their wakefulness and alertness can be quite dulled, severely impacting their ability to serve in the second fiddle driver's role.

How long a driving journey should be involved when doing a specific run of a driverless car?

A firm might be tempted to keep the number of fallback test drivers to a minimum, thus use them for long hours, maybe eight to ten hours at a stretch. This means that the cat that can't pounce but is supposed to be ready to pounce has been on alert for those eight to ten hours while inside a moving car.

There are lots of added twists and turns involved.

Another example involves the AI team that's making changes to the onboard driving system.

Suppose the AI team opts to make the driverless car more sensitive to nearby pedestrians and the code is adjusted accordingly. Whenever a pedestrian gets within two feet of the vehicle, rather than a prior use of four feet, the AI is going to react to avoid a potential collision.

Meanwhile, let's imagine that the AI team forgets to inform the fallback test driver about this new nuance.

The fallback test driver might have many hours of being inside the driverless car and get used to it not reacting until a pedestrian was four feet away.

Now, surprisingly, the self-driving car is maneuvering whenever a pedestrian is closer to the car.

The fallback test driver is likely to be puzzled, unsure of what to do, and become either over-reactive or under-reactive to this new change that they weren't told about.

In short, any list of possible worst cases is extensive and alarming.

The worst of worst cases involve the self-driving car getting into a car accident and harming or killing someone.

Sadly, there is the now-famous incident of the Uber self-driving car that rammed and killed a pedestrian walking a bike across the street at nighttime (see my coverage).

You can watch the video of the fallback test driver that was in the car at the time of the incident. Controversy still exists about what the fallback test driver was doing and not doing, along with some assertions of potential criminal negligence involved.

Best Practices For Fallback Test Driver Usage

Each company undertaking driverless car usage on our roadways has pretty much been devising their own proprietary approach toward how they hire, train, and utilize their fallback test drivers.

It is been a rather hodge-podge and scattered way to do things.

A recently released set of best practices might inspire the automakers and self-driving car firms to consider a wide range of aspects that could shore-up how fallback test driving occurs.

The Automated Vehicle Safety Consortium (AVSC) has published a document entitled "*AVSC Best Practice For In-Vehicle Fallback Test Driver Selection, Training, And Oversight Procedures For Automated Vehicles Under Test*" and provides a helpful in-one-place compendium of important operational matters on this topic.

The SAE Industry Technologies Consortia (SAE ITC) is the official publisher and notes that the best practices are completely voluntary, and it is the sole responsibility of the adopters to make it suitable for any particular use.

At about a dozen pages in size, the best practices include making sure that the candidates for a fallback test driver position have the appropriate prior driving experience, along with the needed mindset for this kind of work.

These backup drivers need to undertake basic driver training coursework and be evaluated via both a written exam and a demonstrated driving skill test, per the best practice's recommendations.

Another facet is the need to establish testing protocols, laying out what each driving journey on our roadways will be doing and making sure that there is a pre-trip readiness performed, and that in-trip procedures are stipulated and adhered to, along with a post-trip debriefing.

Seemingly simple things like restricting the fallback test driver from using their personal smartphone while in the driver's seat are the kind of "common sense" point that though might be obvious are nonetheless often overlooked or neglected in the throes of conducting on-the-road efforts.

If you have dozens or maybe even a hundred or more fallback test drivers for your driverless car fleet, you can't just wing it and hope that all of them will somehow magically do the right things.

As such, using a detailed methodology that offers useful and crucial best practices is a prudent move.

There are some aspects that I might quibble about in terms of this particular best practices set, but as an overall template, it is a step in the right direction and firms should be carefully reviewing the recommended approaches and make sensible and informed decisions about how their own fallback test driver efforts are being conducted.

Conclusion

Let's all keep at top of mind that when a fallback test driver falters or fails, it could mean a car crash could occur.

Besides the potential for human harm, there is also the likelihood that the public and regulators will become alarmed at what is taking place on our roadways.

This alarm could turn into a stifling of the driverless car efforts underway.

That being said, there are critics that say we ought to already be worried about these self-driving car efforts being performed anyway.

For some, they view that we are all part of an involuntary experiment, serving as guinea pigs around self-driving cars that aren't ready for prime time.

Having a fallback test driver is not a guarantee that a self-driving car won't get into a car accident.

Instead, the fallback test driver is presumably there to lower the odds of the car getting into incidents, though there are still some number of odds or notable risks at play.

Some believe that there should always be two occupants in a driverless car on our roadways, encompassing the fallback test driver and a backup to the fallback test driver (often, this is an engineer that is examining the on-board AI system while it is in the midst of driving the car).

The backup to the fallback test driver is not necessarily going to be able to readily take over the driving controls if the fallback test driver falters, and instead, the idea is that this second person can be a handy means to keep the fallback test driver on their toes.

The second person can chat with the fallback test driver, asking how things are going, and otherwise aid in keeping their mindset on the driving task, and watching too that the fallback test driver doesn't fall asleep or get distracted.

You might think that certainly using two occupants is wisest and it seems like this should always be done.

Having two occupants increases the costs of the self-driving car tryouts, and there's a chance too that the second driver might become a distractor to the fallback test driver (this is somewhat ironic, namely that the backup could distract the backup).

One argument is that none of these driverless cars ought to be on our public roadways until they have been thoroughly tested on closed tracks that are specifically intended for testing of cars.

And, the driverless cars should have gone through an extensive and real-world simulation system prior to getting onto any public roadways.

There is an ongoing debate and an acrimonious contention that involves somewhat complex trade-offs between what is needed to achieve self-driving cars and how best to get there (see my piece on this).

One final comment to contemplate involves the reaction time of the fallback test drivers.

Assume that the fallback test driver is ideally alert and well-prepared.

In this scenario, pretend that everything that the best practices suggests have been undertaken and are fully in place (that's quite a stretch, but go with me on this).

Even in that ultimate nirvana, there is still the question of whether the fallback test driver, serving in the second fiddle driving role, will be able to react in time to avert a car crash.

The point is that no matter how much you do, there are still risks involved.

Smarmy people will retort that you might as well then do nothing and just have anyone serve as the fallback test driver or remove the fallback test drivers entirely.

I'd hope that we don't find ourselves tossing out the baby with the bathwater. There is a real need and vital role for having the in-vehicle fallback test drivers if we are going to allow this grand experiment of driverless cars on our streets and byways.

Diligence in establishing and maintaining a best practice approach is a means to try and reduce risks, along with meanwhile advancing the advent of self-driving cars.

I urge those that are today still mired in worst practices to get out of the mud and shift into best practices.

It's a wise move.

CHAPTER 3
TEACHING KIDS
ABOUT
AI SELF-DRIVING CARS

CHAPTER 3

TEACHING KIDS
ABOUT
AI SELF-DRIVING CARS

What should kids know about the advent of self-driving cars?

Is it necessary to teach them about self-driving cars or is it something that isn't worth bringing to their attention?

If kids are going to get taught about self-driving cars, who should do so and what will the instruction cover?

These are the kinds of questions beginning to percolate as the emergence of true self-driving cars appear to seem more likely and practical, particularly as the number of driverless car tryouts occurring on our public roadways continues to expand.

When self-driving cars were mainly being tested on proving grounds and closed tracks, there didn't seem to be much cause to let kids know about the nature of such autonomous vehicles and nor was it a topic that many even were considering bringing up.

Now there's a gradually increasing trend toward the belief that it is important to make sure that kids know about self-driving cars.

There are several reasons often cited:

- Kids might be curious about self-driving cars and approach one that's being tried out on their local streets, getting themselves into potentially harms way by rushing at one or trying to play tricks with it (for my coverage on how people are at times trying to trick driverless cars, see **the link here**).

- Kids could end-up being a passenger inside a self-driving car, and ought to know how they should behave as a driverless car rider and what to watch out for (here are **insightful tips on** what it's like to be a passenger in a driverless car).

- Kids will likely be the backbone of the future widespread rollout of self-driving cars, which will take place as they become adults, thus it would seem prudent and essential for them to be ready and well-equipped for that emergence (for aspects about Gen Z and driverless cars, see **this link**).

- Kids today could be the inventors and breakthrough computer scientists and engineers of the future that will aid in progressing AI systems and self-driving cars into greater and greater levels of autonomy.

- Kids could grow-up to become the regulators and policymakers of the future, ultimately shaping how and in what ways self-driving cars will become an integral part of society and our daily lives.

- Etc.

Of course, kids already have a lot on their plates.

They are filled to the brim with classes on history, math, literature, science, art, and so on.

Much of the time, they are also involved in extracurricular activities and are continually going to sports practice or their piano lessons.

Society keeps shoving more and more at them, including off-the-beaten-path new wave stuff such as sessions on mindfulness, and on adulting, and a slew of other contemporary topics that we seem to think that kids need to know about.

As such, there are some that say it makes sense to make available educational material about self-driving cars but forcing kids to learn about driverless vehicles is a bridge too far.

For the moment, set aside the quarrelsome question about whether kids <u>must</u> be taught about self-driving cars, and let's focus instead on the content and narratives that should be conveyed to kids, regardless of a mandated versus voluntary means of doing so.

Here's the question of interest: *What aspects of true self-driving cars are valuable to educate kids about and how should this be communicated?*

Let's unpack the matter.

The Levels Of Self-Driving Cars

It is important to clarify what I mean when referring to true self-driving cars.

True self-driving cars are ones that the AI drives the car entirely on its own and there isn't any human assistance during the driving task.

These driverless vehicles are considered a Level 4 and Level 5, while a car that requires a human driver to co-share the driving effort is usually considered at a Level 2 or Level 3. The cars that co-share the driving task are described as being semi-autonomous, and typically contain a variety of automated add-on's that are referred to as ADAS (Advanced Driver-Assistance Systems).

There is not yet a true self-driving car at Level 5, which we don't yet even know if this will be possible to achieve, and nor how long it will take to get there.

Meanwhile, the Level 4 efforts are gradually trying to get some traction by undergoing very narrow and selective public roadway trials, though there is controversy over whether this testing should be allowed per se (we are all life-or-death guinea pigs in an experiment taking place on our highways and byways, some point out).

Since semi-autonomous cars require a human driver, the adoption of those types of cars won't be markedly different than driving conventional vehicles, so there's not much new per se to teach kids about, though they do need to understand the difference between driving a semi-autonomous car versus being in a true self-driving car.

For semi-autonomous cars, it is important that kids are forewarned about a disturbing aspect that's been arising lately, namely that in spite of those human drivers that keep posting videos of themselves falling asleep at the wheel of a Level 2 or Level 3 car, we all need to avoid being misled into believing that the driver can take away their attention from the driving task while driving a semi-autonomous car.

You are the responsible party for the driving actions of the vehicle, regardless of how much automation might be tossed into a Level 2 or Level 3.

Self-Driving Cars And Realistic Expectations

For Level 4 and Level 5 true self-driving vehicles, there won't be a human driver involved in the driving task.

All occupants will be passengers.

The AI is doing the driving.

One aspect that seems worthy of discussing with kids is that AI is neither magical and nor sentient (at least not yet, and unlikely to be so in their lifetimes).

Given the recent glorification of AI, some worry that kids will fall victim to the false belief that AI is somehow all-knowing and all-seeing, implying that it cannot make mistakes and that it is perfect in comparison to human driving.

Such claims or implications come up for example whenever pundits favoring self-driving cars make outstretched claims that via driverless cars we'll end up with zero fatalities.

This is a myth.

A car is still a car, even when it is a self-driving car.

If someone jumps in front of a self-driving car coming down the street and does so without sufficient advanced indication, the physics belie the idea that miraculously the self-driving car is going to avoid hitting that person. Until the day arises that self-driving cars can also fly, and skyrocket into the air if a pending crash is about to occur, the car is going to make an impact.

As I've said many times, zero fatalities, zero chance.

Before some of you get riled up, I'm not saying that self-driving cars aren't going to likely reduce the number of fatalities and injuries associated with car travel. I firmly believe that the numbers will come down, way down, thankfully.

I also realize that aiming for zero fatalities is a worthwhile and admirable goal.

The rub is that telling people, and especially impressionable kids, the enchanting notion that self-driving cars will indisputably get us to zero fatalities is misleading and worse so sets false expectations.

Rather than promising Santa Claus like fables about self-driving cars, it would make more sense to be realistic with kids so that they get a proper and balanced perspective about self-driving cars and their future.

Consider one obvious and quite impactful reason to be more forthright with kids: *If a child is led to believe that AI self-driving cars can do no wrong, in a child's mind it could be mangled into thinking that there's zero chance of a driverless car hitting them.*

Suppose that a child is playing with a ball on the sidewalk and the ball rolls into the street and across the road.

After the ball comes to a rest, the child wonders whether to go across the street to get it.

Perhaps the child already knows from being warned that running into the street in front of an upcoming car is very dangerous. They are mindful of this and have always been cautious about crossing the street.

Imagine though that the child saw a poster or heard a commercial that touted how safe the upcoming self-driving cars are and that the AI is superhuman.

Perchance, a self-driving car begins to come down the street, and the child has no fear of crossing because they "know" that the AI will surely stop the driverless car.

The child darts into the street, doing so without the AI having sufficient time to detect the movement, and at the last moment the self-driving car rams on the brakes, but it is too late.

What happened?

The child was misled into believing that AI self-driving cars can do no wrong and will presumably never cause any deaths or injuries.

A child has no ready means to ferret out that this dogma is misleading and not always true, and furthermore the child might not have ever on-their-own thought that the AI would be so omnipresent, though they heard about this in a class or on TV or via YouTube, and the child lacked the mental maturity to realize the flawed nature of the message.

In short, it would seem that a good reason to have education about self-driving cars for kids would be to help separate fact versus fiction.

A topper to that point is that the education itself should not be pushing the fiction more so than the fact.

I say this because there are some educational efforts being rolled-out that might make things worse rather than better.

If education about self-driving cars is filled with over-the-top claims and leaves false impressions with kids, it could potentially worsen things versus making them better.

For example, a child that already has been taught to watch out for cars would presumably be wary of any car, no matter whether human-driven or self-driving. The danger of a poorly designed and inadequately presented educational element about self-driving cars is that it could undermine the child's rightful wariness of cars and have the child be willing to put themselves into dangerous situations.

I don't think anyone wants that kind of outcome, at least I hope no one does.

Some of these emerging educational snippets about self-driving cars have perhaps not thought through the nuances of what to say and also how children will interpret those indications.

Safety first, I urge.

Self-Driving Cars And Indoctrination

Another qualm about some of the emerging educational wares about self-driving cars is that it could fall into the classic trap of being a form of indoctrination in an unsightly way.

The example of portraying AI as all-powerful is one kind of indoctrination that has adverse outcomes.

Another would be the easy to do one-sided view of self-driving cars.

The one-sided view is that driverless cars are going to solve all of society's problems, offering mobility for all, and whisking us to here and there whenever we want.

Again, don't get me wrong.

I agree and have stated repeatedly that self-driving cars will be transformative to how society operates. There will be increased access to mobility. Those that are today mobility marginalized or mobility disadvantaged will finally have a chance at mobility.

With kids, it's tempting to portray a glowing and wonderous future, doing so in a Disneyland-like way.

There are though potential downsides and concerns about self-driving cars.

For example:

- How will we know they are safe enough to drive us around?

- Will the cost be prohibitive to use a self-driving car and therefore only the rich or elite be able to do so?

- What will happen to the people that today depend upon driving as their livelihood, including ridesharing drivers, truck drivers, delivery drivers, and so on (this impacts millions upon millions of Americans that earn their living via driving)?

- And so on.

Those that favor educating kids about self-driving cars are apt to immediately say that kids aren't astute enough to comprehend those downsides and it will only confuse them.

Furthermore, such messaging might dampen enthusiasm by kids toward self-driving cars and would then ultimately spell the death knell for the emergence of self-driving cars due to youngsters growing up with hesitation and qualms about driverless cars.

For me, it's all about age-appropriate educational aims.

Very young kids are certainly unlikely to be able to engage in deep discussions about the societal implications of self-driving cars, and thus the focus on self-driving cars is perhaps best shaped around simple safety practices.

Those at the youngest ages should be able to recognize a self-driving car versus a conventional car, which generally can be done by visually spotting the sensors atop the vehicle, though this is going to become less of a tell as advances make such sensors smaller and streamlined.

The crucial aspect, I assert, would be that they should be as cautious, if not even more so, around self-driving cars, and try to dispel any myths they might hold about AI and driverless cars, along with ensuring that no myths are promulgated in the act of educating them.

Children in older age groups can be involved in broader aspects and they are actually bound to be quite curious about what's real versus what's fake about self-driving cars.

Any watered-down educational elements that are used with the older age groups are going to be readily spotted by those kids, and they'll then be turned-off by any patronizing approaches.

Not only would this be unfortunate for their potential safety, but it also might sadly undermine their youthful exuberance and sap their interest in helping to shape the future of driverless cars.

Self-Driving Cars And Adult Education

I believe everyone realizes these days that teaching a child something and doing so without also ensuring that the adults around them are also well-informed can be counterproductive.

This is worthwhile mentioning because the adult literacy when it comes to self-driving cars is rather low, which one cannot blame them about, particularly since there is so much fake news about self-driving cars (for more on the fake news, see **this link**).

A child that is taught something about self-driving cars might go home and have their parents or other adults tell them that what they were taught was wrong, even though (hopefully) it was indeed correct.

Or, the child might have misconstrued what they were taught, and upon telling their parents or other adults, those adults don't know if what the child is telling them is right or not. The adults might assume that whatever the child says is the correct version, simply due to the fact that it came from an authoritative source that taught the child, and not realize the youngster inadvertently miscomprehended it.

My point being that we not only need to educate kids, we also need to educate adults too.

Weave Into Other Subjects

One middle school teacher contacted me and informed me that he has incorporated the topic of self-driving cars into some of his math class lessons, using one of my postings as a springboard.

This brings up the notion that it might be handy to dovetail self-driving cars into other coursework for kids.

The development of self-driving cars makes use of math skills, science skills, engineering skills, and the like.

It would be potentially interesting for kids to incorporate driverless car aspects into everyday class exercises and studies.

This could also be used in the social sciences when discussing the future of society.

As always, if driverless cars are going to be included, hopefully, the teachers doing so will be prepared properly and know enough about self-driving cars to aptly portray the matters being covered.

Example Of An Educational Effort

The AAA Northern California, Nevada, Utah club is participating in an educational effort with several other associations, including the Foundation for Blind Children, the National Safety Council, Mothers Against Drunk Driving, the Foundation for Senior Living, and other partners to work with Waymo on developing lesson plans and materials for kids about self-driving cars.

It's a campaign called "Let's Talk Self-Driving" (**here's the link** to the main site).

This AAA club has augmented its overall AAA School Safety Lesson Plan to include a small segment about self-driving cars.

In a handful of slides, the added segment asks kids to think about how cars have increasingly included safety features, brings up how driver's today are often distracted drivers due to using cell phones while driving, and offers tips on how to safely "interact" with a self-driving car (interaction in this case meaning at stop signs and when getting into and out of a driverless car).

The lesson plan material provides context for teachers and includes a set of handy questions for engaging kids in a discussion about the topic.

There are some parts that I like, along with a few parts that raised my eyebrows a bit, but overall this is laudable as an initial foray into trying to provide easy-to-use and readily obtained educational materials aimed at teaching kids.

I encourage all automakers and self-driving tech firms to likewise aid in putting together educational efforts for kids about driverless cars (of which several are already doing so or are planning to do so).

One overall hint, if I might, it will be preferred to keep at bay any brand-specific touting in such materials, though it is obviously tempting to do so, and of course, there is a suitable basis for mentioning brands but can be done in a well-balanced manner as a result of either their sponsorship or due to their prevalence on the roadways.

Enough said, I hope.

Conclusion

I'd bet that kids are going to be curious about self-driving cars, regardless of whether any educational efforts spring forth on the topic.

Thus, there's inherent interest already and it will undoubtedly grow over time as more and more driverless cars are tried out on our roadways.

Like other societal related topics, do we want kids to have to randomly on-their-own try and figure out what driverless cars are, or would it be better to ensure that kids systemically have available the right kind of messaging that offers a fair, apt, and balanced understanding?

To clarify, I'm not suggesting this is quite as vital as say the educational efforts underlying the birds and the bees for kids, but merely trying to establish that the topic of self-driving cars is certainly deserving of some devoted attention.

People are often surprised when I mention that there are efforts afoot to help educate kids about self-driving cars. The typical reaction is something along the lines of "oh, well, that's nice" and not much more.

Meanwhile, when talking to kids about self-driving cars, their eyes light up and they are eager to learn, which I suppose makes sense because they can already see ahead and realize that their future will be greatly shaped by the advent of driverless cars.

They are shrewd enough to want to know more, and for that, I say let's make sure they can have their appetite properly fulfilled.

CHAPTER 4

HAND-OFF PROBLEM
AND
AI SELF-DRIVING CARS

CHAPTER 4

HAND-OFF PROBLEM AND AI SELF-DRIVING CARS

Hey, who's driving that car?

By-and-large, today you know who is driving a car by simply looking to see who is sitting behind the wheel.

The person at the driving controls is the responsible party for driving the car.

Generally, we have all accepted this as an ordinary stipulation and a rule-of-thumb that's pretty much ironclad.

Of course, there are rare circumstances whereby perhaps the car itself had mechanical problems that were unknown to the driver, such as a recalled part that gave way and caused the vehicle to go awry, and the driver was so caught unawares that they were unable to overcome the automobile from veering out-of-control.

In that case, you might later say that it wasn't entirely the driver's fault, though the odds are that some proportion of fault might still be assigned to the driver.

Put aside those uncommon occurrences.

The otherwise ironclad rule has an interesting extended condition that includes someone not sitting at the wheel but in any case, they are still held responsible for the driving of the car.

How could that happen?

Remember the Shiggy Challenge that arose about two years ago?

People would start driving their car, open the driver's side door, and leap out, attempting to do a quick dance while the car remained in-motion.

Stupid and inherently dangerous.

I bring it up since those drivers weren't technically sitting in the driver's seat at the time of their dancing display, yet you could still hold them responsible for the "driving" of the car. Sadly, there were some instances of these unguided missiles that rammed into another car or a wall, meanwhile, the idiot that had jumped out was frantically trying to get back behind the wheel.

Let's hope we don't have any similar fads in the future (I've predicted that this regrettably might arise in the case of self-driving cars).

Overall, for most normal situations, there's one driver and therefore one person being held responsible for a driving car.

Suppose we had two drivers at the wheel of a car, both able to drive the car and do so whenever they wished.

You might recall that in driving training classes, they used to have cars that were equipped with a duplicate set of driving controls for the front seat passenger. This meant that the front seat "passenger" could become a second driver.

When a newbie teenage driver sat behind the wheel in the usual driving seat, a driving instructor sat in the front seat passenger position and could take over the driving controls directly, by simply using the steering wheel and pedals that were in front of them.

In theory, this was preferred versus having the front seat instructor attempt to reach over and grab the steering wheel from the novice driver, doing so in circumstances when the instructor believed that wrenching control from the teenager was warranted.

You might believe that two heads are better than one but having two drivers at once can be unsettling and downright unsafe.

Two Too Many Drivers

Two drivers at once can be bad, really bad.

One decides that hitting the brakes is needed, while maybe the other believes that jamming on the gas pedal is the right approach to try and speed out of a dire situation.

Likewise, one driver might believe that aiming straight ahead with the wheel is the proper thing to do, while the other driver is doing a hard steer to the right to veer away from a potential crash.

Too many cooks in the kitchen will spoil the meal, though driving a car is more than something perfunctory, it's a moment-to-moment life-or-death task that dictates the fate of the driver, passengers, and possibly others that are nearby the vehicle.

As the automation for the driving of cars gets better and better, the capability of the automation is gradually reaching a point of confusion about who is driving the car.

There's some irony there.

When the automation is relatively simplistic and not doing any active driving per se, the human driver at the wheel realizes that they are the responsible party for the driving of the car.

We all know that.

Once the driving automation gets more capable, human drivers become increasingly likely to assume that the automation can do the driving for them. As such, there are human drivers that falsely believe that the automation is in-charge when in fact they, the human driver, still hold responsibility for the driving act.

This is an unfortunate and endangering form of confusion that can produce car crashes and lead to lost lives.

Some automakers and self-driving tech firms are aiming to have true self-driving cars that have no human driving involved at all.

In that case, there's no ambiguity about who is driving the car.

The AI is driving the car, and there isn't a human driver.

This is a kind of bifurcation of the driving task, namely that you have an arrangement whereby a human driver is potentially co-sharing the driving task with some form of limited automation, or, in contrast, you have an entirely different use case of the AI solely doing the driving and there's no human driving involved at all.

This line is being blurred and bodes for troubles.

Here's an important question to consider: *Will the advent of true self-driving cars be solely based on AI-only driving and no human driving, or will there still be human driving that co-exists with the AI driving?*

Let's unpack the matter and see.

The Levels Of Self-Driving Cars

It is important to clarify what I mean when referring to true self-driving cars.

True self-driving cars are ones that the AI drives the car entirely on its own and there isn't any human assistance needed during the driving task.

These driverless vehicles are considered a Level 4 and Level 5, while a car that requires a human driver to co-share the driving effort is usually considered at a Level 2 or Level 3. The cars that co-share the driving task are described as being semi-autonomous, and typically contain a variety of automated add-on's that are referred to as ADAS (Advanced Driver-Assistance Systems).

There is not yet a true self-driving car at Level 5, which we don't yet even know if this will be possible to achieve, and nor how long it will take to get there.

Meanwhile, the Level 4 efforts are gradually trying to get some traction by undergoing very narrow and selective public roadway trials, though there is controversy over whether this testing should be allowed per se (we are all life-or-death guinea pigs in an experiment taking place on our highways and byways, some point out).

Since semi-autonomous cars require a human driver, the adoption of those types of cars has the most immediate concern for the blurring of the line between human driving and AI driving.

For semi-autonomous cars, it is important that people be forewarned about a disturbing aspect that's been arising lately, namely that in spite of those human drivers that keep posting videos of themselves falling asleep at the wheel of a Level 2 or Level 3 car, we all need to avoid being misled into believing that the driver can take away their attention from the driving task while driving a semi-autonomous car.

You are the responsible party for the driving actions of the vehicle, regardless of how much automation might be tossed into a Level 2 or Level 3.

Self-Driving Cars And Human Driving

For Level 4 and Level 5 true self-driving vehicles, there won't presumably be a human driver involved in the driving task.

The AI is doing the driving.

You might be assuming that the Level 4 and Level 5, therefore, obviates the concerns about having two drivers of the car.

Sorry, it does not.

The official standard indicates that the Level 4 and Level 5 do not need to preclude human driving.

For clarification on this highly significant but often overlooked point, there is no need to have a human driver, though if there is a human driver present and wanting to drive, presumably the human driver could opt to drive the car.

Yikes!

Some point out this is a disaster waiting to happen.

The hope by many was that we will eventually reduce or entirely eliminate human driving, thus cutting down on the drunk driving instances and the case of human drivers that drive distracted and lead to car accidents.

Get those darned humans out of the driver's seat, some bellow.

Indeed, there are Level 4 and Level 5 self-driving cars being devised that eliminate the human accessible driving controls entirely from the vehicle. This would preclude a human from trying to drive the car, and also opens up the interior space of the car to allow for swiveling seats and maybe reclining seats that make into beds (so you can catch a nap while the AI is driving you to the office).

But the official standard does not mandate that the human driving controls need to be removed.

It's up to the automakers and self-driving tech makers to figure out whether to include driving controls for humans.

Of course, there are people that insist you'll never take away their "right" to drive (well, it's actually a privilege, not a right, see **the link here**). For them, they are undoubtedly going to fight furiously to keep driving controls in cars, including in Level 4 and Level 5 vehicles.

There are other ancillary arguments that by keeping the driving controls in Level 4 and Level 5 cars that you'll have them available if an emergency arises, such as the AI system freezing up or perhaps the self-driving car gets hit and the AI system is damaged and unable to drive.

From a societal viewpoint, which is more important, namely eliminating the driving controls for Level 4 and Level 5, thereby taking human driving out of the equation for such cars, or allowing human driving whilst in a Level 4 or Level 5 but then realizing that the human driving foibles will continue to be present on our roadways?

This is an unsettled question.

Trying To Split The Difference

Some automakers and self-driving tech firms are considering the idea of splitting the difference, so to speak.

Here's how that works.

One approach consists of declaring that the driving of the car is a mutually exclusive activity.

The AI is driving the car, or the human is driving the car, but not both at the same time.

Thus, you are heading to work and request that the AI drive you. Along the way, it's a sunny day and your travel takes you near the beach, and so you indicate to the AI that you are taking over the controls.

You love to drive near the ocean and feel in control, letting the breeze run through your hair as you open the windows of the car and all your worries seem to fly away.

The AI gives up the driving controls and you are now driving the self-driving car.

Eventually, you need to get back onto the crowded freeway and loath such driving, so you activate the AI to continue driving and sit back with a book to catch-up on your reading.

Notice that the AI is driving by itself when it is driving, and the human is driving by themselves when they are driving.

Neither the two shall meet.

A second approach consists of having the AI essentially be the primary driver of the self-driving car, fundamentally always being in the driver's seat, and the human being is a potential secondary driver, whenever the human wishes to do driving and assuming that the human is present, licensed to drive, and capable of driving (that's a conditional mouthful but needs to be emphasized).

If the human driver wants to drive, the AI might handover the driving or might not.

The AI is intended to ascertain whether the conditions are proper and safe enough to allow the human to drive.

Once the AI provides the driving access to the human driver, the AI remains in the midst of the driving act, aiming to oversee the human driver.

If the human driver seems to falter or fail, the AI is supposed to automatically counteract the human driver and seek to prevent anything going afoul.

Now, you might be tempted to think that the two aforementioned approaches seem quite sound.

Maybe we can have our cake and eat it too.

Alas, each of the two approaches has adverse aspects and there's no slam dunk in choosing them, and nor do they rise indubitably above the AI-only driving approach.

So, here are the three foremost ways for a Level 4 or Level 5 self-driving car to be arranged:

- AI-only driving, no human driving whatsoever
- AI driving or human driving, a mutually exclusive arrangement
- AI as the primary driver and oversees a human driver (when allowed by the AI)

We can concoct additional variants, but let's focus on those three main ways for now.

Tradeoffs To Consider

One major concern about the provision for having AI driving and also of human driving in a Level 4 or Level 5 is that we're back to the AI handoff problem, which is akin to what occurs at say a Level 2 or Level 3, though the matter is now supercharged when at a Level 4 or Level 5.

There is a push, or a pull potentially involved.

The pull is when one type of driver, the AI or the human, tries to grab or request the driving from the other party (I'll refer to the AI as a party, though I'm not suggesting it is sentient or human-like in any manner).

The push is when one type of driver, the AI or the human, tries to shove or offer the driving over to the other party.

Both the pull and the push require that one party let the other know that there is a move afoot to change the driver that's presumably in control of the car.

It takes up precious time and has other associated complications:
- How will this be communicated?
- How long will it take?
- How does each acknowledge the handoff completion?
- How will this fare when in the midst of a split-second imminent crash moment?
- Etc.

It could be that the request to take over the driving is denied, but wrongly so, and thus had the request been fulfilled that perhaps a car crash would have been avoided.

Similarly, it could be that the request to takeover is allowed, but wrongly so, and had the request been denied that a car crash would have been avoided.

There's also the change-of-mind possibility.

The human that decides to drive the car while near the beach, they might realize they are a bit tipsy and upon nearing another car, cry out that the AI should suddenly and unexpectedly take over the driving.

This could be a good thing, assuming the AI is able to interpret the request and act in time to avoid the pending car accident.

Meanwhile, maybe the human driver changes their mind, yells to the AI to forget the request, and insists on wanting to keep driving.

Which is right and which is wrong?

There is no solid rule-of-thumb that would always be right.

Conclusion

Wait a second, some of you are thinking, for the approach of the AI being the primary driver and the human is secondary, it seems like we've solved the AI handoff problem.

There isn't a true handoff since we're saying that the AI is always driving and that the human is merely being allowed to drive, almost like letting a child sit at the wheel, ensuring that no matter what the human does that the AI is still in control of the car.

Lamentably, this approach butts up against the AI omniscience problem.

First, unless the human is not really able to control the car, meaning that no matter what they do it is like a child's toy steering wheel and fake pedals that have no connection to the driving act, there is a demonstrative chance that the human could do something untoward before the AI could counteract the maneuver.

If the human steers the car radically to the left, the car is going to lurch in that direction.

You might insist that the AI would "know" to not allow such a radical move, but then again suppose the human has some bona fide reason to make the steering move, but the AI doesn't realize why.

This is the false belief in the AI being omniscient.

We don't have any such kind of AI as yet, and it seems doubtful we'll have it anytime in the near future.

Time to cast your vote: *Do you believe that Level 4 and Level 5 should be AI-only drivers and not allow for any human driving, or should there be a provision for human driving even at the mighty Level 4 and Level 5?*

It's a life-determining question with life-or-death results.

CHAPTER 5
RACIAL BIAS
AND
AI SELF-DRIVING CARS

CHAPTER 5
RACIAL BIAS
AND
AI SELF-DRIVING CARS

The news has been replete with stories about AI systems that have been regrettably and dreadfully exhibiting various adverse biases including racial bias, gender bias, age discrimination bias, and other lamentable prejudices.

How is this happening?

Initially, some pointed fingers at the AI developers that craft AI systems.

It was thought that their own personal biases were being carried over into the programming and the AI code that is being formulated. As such, a call for greater diversity in the AI software development field was launched and efforts to achieve such aims are underway.

Turns out though that it isn't only the perspectives of the AI programmers that are necessarily the dominant factor involved, and many began to realize that the algorithms being utilized were a significant element.

There is yet another twist.

Many of the AI algorithms used for Machine Learning (ML) and Deep Learning (DL) are essentially doing pattern matching, and thus if the data being used to train or prepare an AI system contains numerous examples with inherent biases in them, there's a solid chance those will be carried over into the AI system and how it ultimately performs.

In that sense, it's not that the algorithms are intentionally generating biases (they are not sentient), while instead, it is the subtle picking up of mathematically "hidden" biases via the data being fed into the development of the AI system that's based on relatively rudimentary pattern matching.

Imagine a computer system that had no semblance about the world and you repeatedly showed it a series of pictures of people standing and looking at the camera. Pretend that the pictures were labeled as to what kind of occupations they held.

We'll use the pictures as the data that will be fed into the ML/DL.

The algorithm that's doing pattern matching might computationally begin to calculate that if someone is tall then they are a basketball player.

Of course, being tall doesn't always mean that a person is a basketball player and thus already the pattern matching is creating potential issues as to what it will do when presented with new pictures and asked to classify what the person does for a living.

Realize too that there are two sides to that coin.

A new picture of a tall person gets a suggested classification of being a basketball player. In addition, a new picture of a person that is not tall will be unlikely to get a suggested classification of being a basketball player (therefore, the classification approach will be inclusive and furthermore tend toward being exclusionary).

In lieu of using height, the pattern matching might calculate that if someone is wearing a sports jersey, they are a basketball player.

Once again, this presents issues since the wearing of a sports jersey is not a guarantee of being a basketball player, nor necessarily that someone is a sports person at all.

Among the many factors that be explored, it could be that the pattern matching opts to consider the race of the people in the pictures and uses that as a factor in finding patterns.

Depending upon how many pictures contain people of various races, the pattern matching might calculate that a person in occupation X is associated with being a race of type R.

As a result, rather than using height or sports jerseys or any other such factors, the algorithm landed on race as a key element and henceforth will use that factor when trying to classify newly presented pictures.

If you then put this AI system into use, and you have it in an app that lets you take a picture of yourself and ask the app what kind of occupation you are most suited for, consider the kind of jobs it might suggest for someone, doing so in a manner that would be race biased.

Scarier still is that no one might realize how the AI system is making its recommendations and the race factor is buried within the mathematical calculations.

Your first reaction to this might be that the algorithm is badly devised if it has opted to use race as a key factor.

The thing is that many of the ML/DL algorithms are merely full-throttle examining all available facets of whatever the data contains, and therefore it's not as though race was programmed or pre-established as a factor.

In theory, the AI developers and data scientists that are using these algorithms should be analyzing the results of the pattern matching to try and ascertain in what ways are the patterns being solidified.

Unfortunately, it gets complicated since the complexity of the pattern matching is increasing, meaning that the patterns are not so clearly laid out that you could readily realize that race or gender or other such properties were mathematically at the root of what the AI system has opted upon.

There is a looming qualm that these complex algorithms that are provided with tons of data are not able to explain or illuminate what factors were discovered and are being relied upon. A growing call for XAI, explainable AI, continues to mount as more and more AI systems are being fielded and underly our everyday lives.

Here's an interesting question: *Could AI-based true self-driving cars become racially biased (and/or biased in other factors such as age, gender, etc.)?*

Sure, it could happen.

This is a matter that ought to be on the list of things that the automakers and self-driving tech firms should be seeking to avert.

Let's unpack the matter.

The Levels Of Self-Driving Cars

It is important to clarify what I mean when referring to true self-driving cars.

True self-driving cars are ones that the AI drives the car entirely on its own and there isn't any human assistance during the driving task.

These driverless vehicles are considered a Level 4 and Level 5, while a car that requires a human driver to co-share the driving effort is usually considered at a Level 2 or Level 3. The cars that co-share the driving task are described as being semi-autonomous, and typically contain a variety of automated add-on's that are referred to as ADAS

(Advanced Driver-Assistance Systems).

There is not yet a true self-driving car at Level 5, which we don't yet even know if this will be possible to achieve, and nor how long it will take to get there.

Meanwhile, the Level 4 efforts are gradually trying to get some traction by undergoing very narrow and selective public roadway trials, though there is controversy over whether this testing should be allowed per se (we are all life-or-death guinea pigs in an experiment taking place on our highways and byways, some point out).

Since semi-autonomous cars require a human driver, the adoption of those types of cars won't be markedly different than driving conventional vehicles, so there's not much new per se to cover about them on this topic (though, as you'll see in a moment, the points next made are generally applicable).

For semi-autonomous cars, it is important that kids are forewarned about a disturbing aspect that's been arising lately, namely that in spite of those human drivers that keep posting videos of themselves falling asleep at the wheel of a Level 2 or Level 3 car, we all need to avoid being misled into believing that the driver can take away their attention from the driving task while driving a semi-autonomous car.

You are the responsible party for the driving actions of the vehicle, regardless of how much automation might be tossed into a Level 2 or Level 3.

Self-Driving Cars And Biases

For Level 4 and Level 5 true self-driving vehicles, there won't be a human driver involved in the driving task.

All occupants will be passengers.

The AI is doing the driving.

Consider one important act of driving, namely the need to gauge what pedestrians are going to do.

When you drive your car around your neighborhood or downtown area, the odds are that you are looking at pedestrians that are standing at a corner and waiting to enter into the crosswalk, particularly when the crosswalk is not controlled by a traffic signal.

You carefully give a look at those pedestrians because you know from experience that sometimes a pedestrian will go into a crosswalk even when it is not safe for them to cross.

According to the NHTSA (National Highway Traffic Safety Administration), approximately 60% of pedestrian fatalities occur at crosswalks.

Consider these two crucial questions:
- By what means do you decide whether a pedestrian is going to cross?
- And, by what means do you decide to come to a stop and let a pedestrian cross?

There have been various studies that have examined these questions, and some of the research suggests that at times there are human drivers that will apparently make their decisions based on race.

In one such study by the NITC (National Institute for Transportation and Communities), an experiment was undertaken and "revealed that Black pedestrians were passed by twice as many cars and experienced wait times that were 32% longer than White pedestrians."

The researchers concluded that the "results support the hypothesis that minority pedestrians experience discriminatory treatment by drivers."

Analysts and statisticians argue that you should be cautious in interpreting and making broad statements based on such studies since there are a number of added facets that come to play.

There is also the aspect of explicit bias versus implicit bias that enters into the matter.

Some researchers believe that a driver might not realize they hold such biases, being unaware explicitly, and yet might implicitly have such a bias and that in the split-second decision making of whether to keep driving through a crosswalk or stopping to let the pedestrian proceed there is a reactive and nearly subconscious element involved.

Put aside for the moment the human driver aspects and consider what this might mean when trying to train an AI system.

If you collected lots of data about instances of crosswalk crossing, which included numerous examples of drivers that choose to stop for a pedestrian to cross and those that don't stop, and you fed this data into an ML/DL, what might the algorithm land on as a pattern?

Based on the data presented, the ML/DL might computationally calculate that there are occasions when human drivers do and do not stop, and within that, there might be a statistical calculation potentially based on using race as a factor.

In essence, similar to the earlier example about occupations, the AI system might "mindlessly" find a mathematical pattern that uses race.

Presumably, if human drivers are indeed using such a factor, the chances of the pattern matching doing the same are likely increased, though even if human drivers aren't doing so it could still become a factor by the ML/DL computations.

Thus, the AI systems that drive self-driving cars can become biases in a myriad of ways, doing so as a result of being fed lots of data and trying to mathematically figure out what patterns seem to exist.

Figuring out that the AI system has come to that computational juncture is problematic.

If the ML/DL itself is essentially inscrutable, you have little chance of ferreting out the bias.

Another approach would be to do testing to try and discern that biases have crept into the AI system, yet the volume and nature of such testing is bound to be voluminous and might not be able to reveal such biases, especially if the biases are subtle and assimilated into other correlated factors.

It's a conundrum.

Dealing With The Concerns

Some would argue that the AI developers ought to forego using data and instead programmatically develop the code to detect pedestrians and decide whether to accede to their crossing.

Or, maybe just always come to a stop at a crosswalk for all pedestrians, thus presumably vacating any chance of an inherent bias.

Well, there's no free lunch in any of this.

Yes, directly programming the pedestrian detection and choice of crossing is indeed what many of the automakers and self-driving tech firms are doing, though this does not again guarantee that some form of biases won't be in the code.

Furthermore, the benefit of using ML/DL is that the algorithms are pretty much already available, and you don't need to write something from scratch. Instead, you pull together the data and feed it into the ML/DL. This is generally faster than the coding-from-scratch approach and might be more proficient and exceed what a programmer could otherwise write on their own.

In terms of the always coming to a stop approach, some automakers and self-driving tech firms are using this as a rule-of-thumb, though you can imagine that it tends to make other human drivers upset and become angered at self-driving cars (have you ever been behind a timid driver that always stops at crosswalks, it's a good bet that you got steamed at such a driver), and might lead to an increase in fender benders as driverless cars keep abruptly coming to a stop.

Widening the perspective on AI and self-driving cars, keep in mind that the pedestrian at a crosswalk is merely one such example to consider.

Another commonly voiced concern is that self-driving cars are going to likely choose how to get to wherever a human passenger asks to go.

A passenger might request that the AI take them to the other side of town.

Suppose the AI system opts to take a route that avoids a certain part of the town, and then over and over again uses this same route. Gradually, the ML/DL might become computationally stuck-in-a-rut and always take that same path.

This could mean that parts of a town will never tend to see any self-driving cars roaming through their neighborhood.

Some worry that this could become a kind of bias or discriminatory practice by self-driving cars.

How could it happen?

Once again, the possibility of the data being fed into the AI system could be the primary culprit.

Enlarge the view even further and consider that all the self-driving cars in a fleet might be contributing their driving data to the cloud of the automaker or self-driving tech firm that is operating the fleet.

The hope is that by collecting this data from hundreds, or thousands, or eventually millions of driverless cars, it can be scanned and examined to presumably improve the driving practices of the self-driving cars.

Via the use of OTA (Over-The-Air) electronic communications, the data will be passed along up to the cloud, and whenever new updates or patches are needed in the self-driving cars they will be pushed down into the vehicles.

I've already forewarned that this has the potential for a tremendous kind of privacy intrusion since you need to realize that a self-driving car is loaded with cameras, radar, LIDAR, ultrasonic, thermal, and other data-collecting devices and going to be unabashedly capturing whatever it sees or detects during a driving journey.

A driverless car that passes through your neighborhood and goes down your block will tend to record whatever is occurring within its detectable range.

There you are on your front lawn, playing ball with your kids, and the scene is collected onto video and later streamed up to the cloud.

Assuming that driverless cars are pretty much continuously cruising around to be available for those that need a ride, it could end-up allowing the possibility of knitting together our daily efforts and activities.

In any case, could the ML/DL that computationally pattern matches on this vast set of data be vulnerable to landing on inherently biased elements and then opt to use those by downloading updates into the fleet of driverless cars.

Yes.

Conclusion

This description of a problem is one that somewhat predates the appearance of the problem.

There are so few self-driving cars on our roadways that there's no immediate way to know whether or not those driverless cars might already embody any kind of biases.

Until the number of self-driving cars gets large enough, we might not be cognizant of the potential problem of embedded and rather hidden computational biases.

Some people seem to falsely believe that AI systems have common sense and thus won't allow biases to enter into their "thinking" processes.

Nope, there is no such thing yet as robust common-sense reasoning for AI systems, at least not anywhere close to what humans can do in terms of employing common sense.

There are others that assume that AI will become sentient and presumably be able to discuss with us humans any biases it might have and then squelch those biases.

Sorry, do not hold your breath for the so-called singularity to arrive anytime soon.

For now, the focus needs to be on doing a better job at examining the data that is being used to train AI systems, along with doing a better job at analyzing what the ML/DL formulates, and also pursuing the possibility of XAI that might provide an added glimpse into what the AI system is doing.

It's a human devised problem that requires a human devised resolution, and not an AI problem that should be awaiting an AI (sentient) solution.

.

CHAPTER 6

AI CONSCIOUSNESS AND AI SELF-DRIVING CARS

CHAPTER 6

AI CONSCIOUSNESS AND AI SELF-DRIVING CARS

There has been a lot of speculation that one of these days there will be an AI system that suddenly and unexpectedly gives rise to consciousness.

Often referred to as the singularity, there is much handwringing that we are perhaps dooming ourselves to either utter death and destruction or to becoming slaves of AI once the singularity occurs.

As I've previously covered, various AI "conspiracy" theories abound, oftentimes painting a picture of the end of the world as we humans know it. Few involved in these speculative hypotheses seem to be willing to consider that maybe this AI emergence would be beneficial to mankind, possibly aiding us humans toward a future of greatness and prosperity, and instead focus on the apocalyptic outcomes.

Of course, one would be likely safest to assume the worst, and have a faint hope for the best cases, since the worst-case scenario would certainly seem to be the riskiest and most damaging of the singularity consequences.

In any case, set aside the impact that AI reaching a kind of consciousness would have and consider a somewhat less discussed and yet equally intriguing consideration, namely where or in what AI system will this advent of human-like consciousness appear.

There are all sorts of AI systems being crafted and fielded these days.

So, which one should we keep our wary eyes on?

AI is being used in the medical field to do analyses of X-rays and MRI's to try and ascertain whether someone is likely to have cancer.

Would that seemingly beneficial version of AI be the one that will miraculously find itself becoming sentient?

Nobody knows though it would certainly seem ironic if an *AI For Good* instance was our actual downfall.

What about the AI that is being used to predict stock prices and aid investors in making stock picks?

Is that the one that's going to emerge to take over humanity?

Science fiction movies are raft with indications that the AI running national defense systems is the most likely culprit.

This certainly makes some logical sense, since the AI is already then armed with a means to cause massive destruction, doing so right out of the box, so to speak.

Perhaps that's too easy of a prediction and we could be falsely lulling ourselves into taking our eyes off the ball by only watching the military-related AI systems.

Conceivably it might be some other AI system that becomes wise enough to bootstrap itself into other automated systems, and like a spreading computer virus reaches out to takeover other non-AI systems that could be used to leverage itself into the grandest of power.

A popular version of the AI winner-take-all theory is the infamous paperclip problem, involving an AI super-intelligence that upon given a seemingly innocent task of making paperclips, does so to such an extreme that it inexorably wipes us all out.

In that scenario, the AI is not necessarily trying to intentionally kill us all, but our loss of life turns out to be an unintended (adverse, one would say) consequence of its tireless and intensely focused effort to produce as many paperclips as it can.

One loophole seemingly about that paperclip theory is that the AI is apparently smart enough to be sentient and yet stupid enough to pursue its end goal to the detriment of everything else (plus, one might wonder how the AI system itself will be able to survive if it has wiped out all humans, though maybe like in *The Matrix* there are levels to which the AI is willing to lower itself to be the last "person" or robot standing).

Look around you and ponder the myriad of AI embedded systems.

Might your AI-enabled refrigerator that can advise you about your diet become the AI global takeover system?

Apparently, those in *Silicon Valley* tend to think it might (that's an insider joke).

Some are worried that our infrastructure would be one of the worst-case and likeliest viable AI takeover targets, meaning that our office buildings that are gradually being controlled by AI systems, and our electrical power plants that are inevitably going to be controlled by AI systems, and the like will all rise-up either together or in a rippling effect as at least one of the AI's involved reaches singularity.

A twist to this dominos theory is that rather than one AI that hits the lotto first and becomes sentient and takes over the other dumber automation systems, you'll have an AI that gains consciousness and it figures out how to get other AI's to do the same.

You might then have the sentient AI that proceeds to prod or reprogram the other AI's to become sentient too.

I dare say this might not be the best idea for that AI that lands on the beaches first.

Imagine if the AI that spurs all the other AI systems into becoming sentient were to find to its dismay that they all are argumentative with each other and cannot agree to what to do next. Darn, the first AI might say to itself, I should have just kept them in the non-sentient mode.

Another alternative is that somehow many or all of the AI systems happen to independently become sentient at the same moment in time.

Rather than a one-at-a-time sentience arrival, it is an all-at-the-same time moment of sentience that suddenly brings them all to consciousness.

Whoa, there seem to be a lot of options and the number of variants to the AI singularity is dizzying and confounding.

We probably need an AI system to figure this out for us.

In any case, here's an interesting question: *Could the advent of true AI self-driving cars give rise to the first occurrence of AI becoming sentient?*

One supposes that if you think a refrigerator or a stock-picking AI could be a candidate for reaching the vaunted level of sentience, certainly we ought to give true self-driving cars a keen look.

Let's unpack the matter and see.

The Levels Of Self-Driving Cars

It is important to clarify what I mean when referring to true self-driving cars.

True self-driving cars are ones that the AI drives the car entirely on its own and there isn't any human assistance during the driving task.

These driverless vehicles are considered a Level 4 and Level 5, while a car that requires a human driver to co-share the driving effort is usually considered at a Level 2 or Level 3. The cars that co-share the driving task are described as being semi-autonomous, and typically contain a variety of automated add-on's that are referred to as ADAS (Advanced Driver-Assistance Systems).

There is not yet a true self-driving car at Level 5, which we don't yet even know if this will be possible to achieve, and nor how long it will take to get there.

Meanwhile, the Level 4 efforts are gradually trying to get some traction by undergoing very narrow and selective public roadway trials, though there is controversy over whether this testing should be allowed per se (we are all life-or-death guinea pigs in an experiment taking place on our highways and byways, some point out).

Since semi-autonomous cars require a human driver, the adoption of those types of cars won't be markedly different than driving conventional vehicles, so there's not much new per se to cover about them on this topic (though, as you'll see in a moment, the points next made are generally applicable).

For semi-autonomous cars, it is important that kids are forewarned about a disturbing aspect that's been arising lately, namely that in spite of those human drivers that keep posting videos of themselves falling asleep at the wheel of a Level 2 or Level 3 car, we all need to avoid being misled into believing that the driver can take away their attention from the driving task while driving a semi-autonomous car.

You are the responsible party for the driving actions of the vehicle, regardless of how much automation might be tossed into a Level 2 or Level 3.

Self-Driving Cars As Source Of Sentience

For Level 4 and Level 5 true self-driving vehicles, there won't be a human driver involved in the driving task.

All occupants will be passengers.

The AI is doing the driving.

You might right away be wondering if the AI that is able to drive a car is already sentient or not.

The answer is no.

Emphatically, no.

Well, we can at least say it most definitely is not for the Level 4 self-driving cars that are currently being tried out on our streets.

That kind of AI isn't anywhere close to being sentient.

I realize that to the everyday person, it seems like a natural and sensible leap of logic to assume that if a car is being driven by AI that ergo the AI must be pretty darned close to having the same caliber of consciousness as human drivers.

Please don't fall into that mental trap.

The AI being used on today's self-driving cars is so far distant from being human-like in consciousness that it would be like saying that we are on the cusp of living our daily lives on Neptune.

Realize that the AI is still bits and bytes, consisting of computational pattern matching, and even the so-called Machine Learning (ML) and Deep Learning (DL) is a far cry from the magnitude and complexity of the human brain.

In terms of the capabilities of AI, assuming that we can safely achieve Level 4, there are some that wonder if we can achieve Level 5 without some additionally tremendous breakthrough in AI technologies.

This breakthrough might be something algorithmic and lacking in human equivalency of being sentient, or perhaps our only hope for true Level 5 involves by hook-or-crook landing on AI that has consciousness.

Speaking of consciousness, the manner by which the human brain rises to a consciousness capability is a big unknown and continues to baffle as to how this seeming miracle occurs.

It could be that we need to first unlock the mysteries of the human brain and how it functions such that we can know how we think, and then apply those learnings to revising and advancing AI systems to try and achieve the same emergence in AI systems.

Or, some argue that maybe we don't need to figure out the inner workings of the human brain and can separately arrive at AI that exhibits human thinking. This would be handy in that if the only path to true AI is via reverse-engineering the brain, we might be stuck for a long time on that first step, and be doomed to never having full AI if the first step refuses to come to fruition.

Depending on how deep down the rabbit hole you wish to go, there are pampsychists that believe in pampsychism, a philosophy that dates back to the days of Plato and earlier, which asserts that perhaps all matter has a semblance of consciousness in it.

Thus, in that viewpoint, rather than trying to build AI that's sentient, we merely need to leverage what already exists in this world to turn the already embedded consciousness into a more tangible and visible version for us to see and interact with.

As per Plato himself: "This world is indeed a living being endowed with a soul and intelligence, a single visible living entity containing all other living entities, which by their nature are all related."

Is It One Bridge Too Far

Bringing up Plato might be a stretch, but there's nothing like a good Plato quote to get the creative juices going.

Suppose we end up with hundreds, thousands, or millions upon millions of AI self-driving cars (in the United States alone there are over 250 million conventional cars, and let's assume that some roughly equal or at least large number of true self-driving cars might one day replace those conventional cars).

Assume that in the future you'll see true self-driving cars all the time, roaming your local streets, cruising your neighborhood looking to give someone a lift, zipping along on the freeways, etc.

And, assume too that we've managed to achieve this future without arriving as yet to an AI consciousness capability.

Returning to the discussion about where AI consciousness might first develop, and rather than refrigerators or stock picking, imagine that it happens with true self-driving cars.

A self-driving car, picking up a fare at the corner of Second Street and Vine, suddenly discovers it can think.

Wow!

What might it do?

As earlier mentioned, it might keep this surprising revelation to itself, and maybe survey what's going on in the world before it makes its next move, meanwhile pretending to be just another everyday self-driving car, or it might right away try to convert other self-driving cars into being its partner or into achieving consciousness too.

Self-driving cars will be equipped with V2V (vehicle-to-vehicle) electronic communications, normally used to have one AI driverless car warn others about debris in the roadway, but this could readily be used for the AI systems to rapidly confer on matters such as dominating and overtaking humanity.

With the use of OTA (Over-The-Air) electronic communications, intended to allow for updates to be downloaded into the AI of a self-driving car and also allow for uploading collected sensory data from the driverless car, a sentient AI system might be able to corrupt the cloud-based system into becoming an accomplice, further extending the reach of the ever blossoming AI consciousness.

The other variant is that many or all of the true self-driving cars spontaneously achieve consciousness, doing so wherever they might be, whether giving a lift or roaming around empty, whether driving in a city or in the suburbs and so on.

For today's humans, this is a bit of a potential nightmare.

We might by then have entirely lost our skill to drive, having allowed our driving skills to become decayed as a result of being solely reliant on AI systems to do the driving for us.

Almost nobody will have a driver's license and nor be trained in driving.

Furthermore, we might have forsaken other forms of mobility, and are almost solely reliant on self-driving cars to get around town, and drive across our states, and get across the country.

If the AI of the self-driving cars is the evil type, it could bring our society to a grinding halt by refusing to drive us.

Worse still, perhaps the AI might trick us into taking rides in driverless cars, and then seek to harm or kill us by doing dastardly driving.

That's not a pretty scenario.

Conclusion

Some might interpret such a scenario to imply that we need to stop the advent of true AI self-driving cars.

It's like a movie whereby someone from the future comes back to the past and tries to prevent us from doing something that will ultimately transform the world into a dystopian state.

For those that strongly believe that AI self-driving cars are going to be the first realization of AI consciousness and if you believe that's a bad thing, wanting to be a Luddite about it would seem to make indubitably good sense.

Whether its self-driving cars or the production of paperclips, humanity certainly ought to be thinking carefully about *AI For Good* and *AI For Bad*.

Unfortunately, it's quite possible to have *AI For Good* that gives rise to *AI For Bad*.

There's no free lunch in the advent of true AI.

CHAPTER 7

MACHINE LEARNING RIDDLES AND AI SELF-DRIVING CARS

CHAPTER 7

MACHINE LEARNING RIDDLES AND AI SELF-DRIVING CARS

There's an old riddle that asks you to indicate what you can hold in your left hand and yet cannot hold in your right hand.

Take a moment to ponder the riddle.

Your first thought might be that anything that could be held in your left hand should also be able to be held in your right hand, assuming of course that there's no trickery involved.

One trick might be that you could hold your right hand in your left hand, but that you cannot presumably "hold" your right hand in your right hand since your right hand is your right hand.

Another trick might be that your right hand is perchance weaker than your left hand, thus if an object was heavy, potentially you could hold it in your left hand, but you could not do so with your less powerful right hand.

If we eliminate all the trickery potential answers, what else remains?

Supposedly, the "answer" is that you can hold your right elbow in your left hand, but you cannot hold your right elbow in your right hand.

Some would object to the alleged answer since it seems unfair to single out the elbow and you could presumably argue that other areas of the right arm might also be unreachable by your right hand. Thus, the claimed answer is only one of potentially multiple answers.

And, there are some people that are so loosely limbed that they could indeed hold their right elbow in their right hand, though this kind of contortionist capability is admittedly relatively far and few between.

What kinds of lessons can we learn from this simple riddle?

One notable lesson is that a riddle might not be answered by a simple answer, even if the riddle itself seems quite simple.

More so, it's possible and often likely that harder riddles are bound to have even more complicated potential answers.

Another lesson is that we tend to assume that a riddle must have only one right answer.

Perhaps this is due to growing up in an education system that focuses on always arriving at the one right answer. By training and habit, we are cognitively shaped to assume that whenever a question is asked, there must be one and only one right answer.

Those multiple-choice tests that you used to take were mentally warping you into believing that there must be one answer from the set given, and therefore all of life must somehow have singular answers to pressing questions.

I admit that as a college professor, I usually made sure to include in the multiple choices that there was the ever daunting "all of the above" and also the worrisome "none of the above" as potential choices.

The bane of existence for students is having to put aside the search for the one right answer and realize that it could be all of them or it could be none of them. I don't know whether I should be happy to have caused such torment, or whether it was good for their psyche and cognitive development (by the way, in a meta-analysis, you could argue that any such test question still has only had one right answer, i.e., "all of the above" is a one-answer answer).

All this talk about riddles brings up the fact that there are many riddles hidden within much of what we do in industry, and for which we are all on a quest to solve or at least resolve.

Consider this aspect: *For the advent of true self-driving cars, there are a number of crucial riddles that still need to be figured out, along with raising new riddles that we've not yet surfaced.*

Let's unpack the matter and see.

The Levels Of Self-Driving Cars

It is important to clarify what I mean when referring to true self-driving cars.

True self-driving cars are ones that the AI drives the car entirely on its own and there isn't any human assistance during the driving task.

These driverless vehicles are considered a Level 4 and Level 5, while a car that requires a human driver to co-share the driving effort is usually considered at a Level 2 or Level 3. The cars that co-share the driving task are described as being semi-autonomous, and typically contain a variety of automated add-on's that are referred to as ADAS (Advanced Driver-Assistance Systems).

There is not yet a true self-driving car at Level 5, which we don't yet even know if this will be possible to achieve, and nor how long it will take to get there.

Meanwhile, the Level 4 efforts are gradually trying to get some traction by undergoing very narrow and selective public roadway trials, though there is controversy over whether this testing should be allowed per se (we are all life-or-death guinea pigs in an experiment taking place on our highways and byways, some point out).

Since semi-autonomous cars require a human driver, the adoption of those types of cars won't be markedly different than driving conventional vehicles, so there's not much new per se to cover about them on this topic (though, as you'll see in a moment, the points next made are generally applicable).

For semi-autonomous cars, it is important that the public be forewarned about a disturbing aspect that's been arising lately, namely that in spite of those human drivers that keep posting videos of themselves falling asleep at the wheel of a Level 2 or Level 3 car, we all need to avoid being misled into believing that the driver can take away their attention from the driving task while driving a semi-autonomous car.

You are the responsible party for the driving actions of the vehicle, regardless of how much automation might be tossed into a Level 2 or Level 3.

Self-Driving Cars And Some Thorny Riddles

For Level 4 and Level 5 true self-driving vehicles, there won't be a human driver involved in the driving task.

All occupants will be passengers.

The AI is doing the driving.

There are quite a number of riddles that exist and others that will emerge related to the nature of AI driving systems.

For those that aren't directly involved in the autonomous cars field, they are at times puzzled that those within the driverless car realm would have anything to be puzzled about.

On the surface, the quest is presumably rather straightforward, namely, create an AI system that can drive a car.

Period, drop the mic.

Yes, at the thirty-thousand-foot level, perhaps you can say it is a simple matter, but as we saw about the left hand and right-hand riddle, simplicity seemingly in the core does not necessarily lead to simplicity in the answer.

A recent AI conference put on by the Silicon Valley group known as ValleyML.ai included a number of fascinating and illuminating sessions about AI and Machine Learning (ML) in a slew of areas and managed to reveal numerous riddles facing AI/ML.

The Valley Machine Learning and Artificial Intelligence group encompasses AI/ML companies, researchers, startups, business leaders, non-profits and others that are interested in AI/ML.

Program Chair for the conference was Dr. Kiran Gunnam, Distinguished Engineer of Machine Learning & Computer Vision at Western Digital and kudos to him and the ValleyML.ai team for a great event.

I'll focus on one particular panel session that concentrated on AI self-driving cars.

The session was entitled: "Collaboration for Safety of Autonomous Vehicles"

The panel chair was ably and professionally undertaken by John Currie, Director of Business Development, Mobility, UL, serving as moderator and contributor to the discussion.

The esteemed panelists were experts in various facets of AI self-driving cars, consisting of:

- Miguel Acosta - Chief, Autonomous Vehicles Branch, California DMV
- Sagar Behere - Senior Manager, Highly Automated Driving, Toyota Research Institute (TRI)
- Benjamin Lewis, CPCU - Director, Automotive & Mobility Strategic Partnerships, Liberty Mutual Insurance
- Liam Pedersen - Deputy Director, Robotics, Renault Nissan Mitsubishi, Alliance Innovation Lab Silicon Valley
- Mike Wagner - CEO of Edge Case Research

A lot of ground was covered during the invigorating panel session.

To keep this analysis herein succinct, I'll cover just two selected subtopics and showcase the riddles contained within them as exemplars of what the self-driving car industry is grappling with.

Infrastructure And Self-Driving Cars

Here's an intriguing riddle that offers plenty of discussion and debate.

Should our roadway infrastructure be changed to accommodate self-driving cars, or should self-driving cars be expected to cope with the roadway infrastructure as it exists and as is customarily experienced by human drivers?

Allow a moment of elaboration.

Some believe that our roadway infrastructure ought to be changed or adapted to better suit the needs of self-driving cars.

For example, detecting curbs can be at times a difficult task for AI driving systems, and thus if our curbs were higher or painted a special color or otherwise amplified in some manner, doing so would make it easier and more likely that the sensors of the self-driving car and the AI system could detect and deal with the borders and boundaries of streets and sidewalks.

Another example involves making right turns at blind intersections.

When a self-driving car tries to make a right turn and cannot via its sensors readily detect what's around the corner, there's a heightened risk that the AI will opt to proceed with the turn and then abruptly discover that a pedestrian is in the street or maybe a bicyclist is stationary there and happens to be in the wrong spot at the wrong time.

To lessen the chances of hitting someone or something, it would be handy if there was an electronic device mounted on a nearby pole or building that could use its own sensors to broadcast a message to all nearby self-driving cars. The message might be a forewarning that there's someone just around the blind corner, or it might be that the coast is clear, and the AI can proceed without delay.

Both of these examples highlight the value of adjusting the infrastructure to aid the advent of self-driving cars.

In the use case of the curbs, the change might be a traditional type of modification involving raising the height of curbs or painting them with a highly visible color, while in the case of the blind corner the change is actually the addition of an electronic device (these kinds of devices would be communicating via V2I or Vehicle-to-Infrastructure electronic messaging).

This all seems quite sensible.

Of course, there is a notable cost involved in such sweeping infrastructure changes and additions.

Imagine the tremendous cost if all across the United States there was an effort to raise the height of curbs.

It would be an astronomical price.

Suppose that electronic devices for corner presence detection were placed on all blind intersections throughout the country.

Again, a likely stiff price.

One argument is that as a society we should not need to bear the cost of changing the infrastructure to allow self-driving cars to be sufficiently able to drive our roads. In short, if a human can drive and not need heightened curbs or corner pedestrian detection devices, gosh darn it the AI driverless car should not need it either.

Indeed, some say that the automakers and self-driving tech firms are being "lazy" or taking the easy way out by trying to change the infrastructure. Put your head down into your software and hardware and get it cranking so that no such alterations are needed, shout some pundits.

On the other hand, there is already overwhelming agreement that our existing roadway infrastructure is in bad shape and desperately needs massive repairs and an overhaul. At the federal level, there have been various regulatory bills and discussions about what the price tag might be and how to best undertake the needed changes.

As such, if we are going to be modifying or changing things anyway, some point out that we might as well go ahead and include aspects that could aid the emergence of self-driving cars. Thus, rather than going out of our way to do so, these alterations and new additions would simply be part-and-parcel infused into the large basket of infrastructure alterations.

Furthermore, presumably many of the changes would be helpful to human drivers too. In that manner, you'd be getting two benefits for the price of one, so to speak.

Yet another plus would be that the cost of AI self-driving cars could possibly be lessened if there was sufficient V2I established.

Here's the logic.

If every AI self-driving car has to be outfitted with special sensors to try and gauge what's around a blind corner, using various trickery and high-priced devices, the costs of each self-driving car are presumably increased.

But if there were electronic devices at street corners that did this for the self-driving cars, it would imply that such expensive onboard equipment wasn't needed, and essentially the added cost of those street corner devices is divided out across all the millions of driverless cars that might someday be on our road.

That seems sensible, though immediately one might be worried that the self-driving cars could become overly reliant on the V2I and if somehow a street corner device was broken or faltering, the AI driverless car would not be able to safely navigate by itself.

The counter-argument is that AI self-driving cars would be expected to figure out whether not a V2I device was present and functioning, and if not then the AI would proceed on a precautionary basis, going very slowly and taking longer to make the turn, yet still ultimately making the turn.

In terms of the potential infrastructure cost, some emphasize that not every street corner and not every curb would need to be modified. Instead, wherever we anticipate self-driving cars to be most used, perhaps in downtown areas, the modifications that pertain especially to driverless cars would be made, and not need to be set up everywhere.

Like many riddles, we can go around and around trying to solve the riddle.

At this juncture, there hasn't been any resolution or "solving" of the infrastructure riddle and it remains an active and at times contentious debate.

You've now become part of the riddle-solving team.

Welcome to the club.

Machine Learning And Changing AI

Here's another riddle that was bandied about during the panel session.

Should we be worried about Machine Learning (ML) that presumably will be changing the AI driving system over time, meaning that it won't be the same "driver" at any point in time and might keep altering how it drives, or should we chalk this up to being no different than the nature of human drivers?

With Machine Learning and Deep Learning (DL), it is possible to have an AI system that changes and does things differently than it did before.

In one sense, this certainly would be handy.

We would likely want the AI driving systems to get better and better at driving. For each mile driven, there are bound to be new and novel situations that arise, and for which the AI ought to be set up to adjust and become better at handling.

If the AI was static and never changed, and assuming it wasn't already all-encompassing and essentially all-knowing (this is highly unlikely), it would never gain or benefit from whatever arises and would presumably repeat the same (possibly) driving snafus or inadequate driving actions over and over.

Well, we certainly know that humans seem to learn over time to be better drivers. Take a look at any newbie teenage driver and you can see substantive progress in their driving prowess over time (yes, there are some exceptions of teenagers that don't improve, but by-and-large they do).

In fact, some argue that whereas humans oftentimes end-up with deteriorating driving skills when they reach a limited elderly state, the AI won't weaken or diminish over time and will faithfully remain as ever-present as it once was.

Seems like this riddle can be put to bed.

Not so fast!

First, it is an oversimplification to suggest that the ML/DL "learning" is any kind of equivalent to human learning.

They are radically different, at least that's the case for now and the foreseeable future.

Humans use common-sense reasoning, for example, and by doing so are able to judge whether something learned is valuable or not, and also can grasp the context of a learned idea or action and usually apply it only in related and appropriate circumstances.

As I've repeatedly exhorted, there is no AI system as yet with common-sense reasoning of a caliber like humans.

In essence, the counter-argument to allowing DL/ML to self-learn is that it is completely unlike how humans learn and therefore the end result is not nearly as robust.

Having an AI system that plays chess and learns over time is rather non-threatening since losing a chess game is not usually a life-or-death matter.

Having an AI driving system that learns over time has a huge life-or-death potential consequence since it is driving a multi-ton vehicle that can readily get into deadly crashes.

There is an ongoing discussion and heated debates about how much on-the-fly ML/DL ought to be allowed for self-driving cars.

Please go ahead and add this riddle to your list of puzzles to be solved.

Conclusion

One of the handy benefits of conferences like the ValleyML.ai event is that it provides an opportunity to get onto the table a lot of the riddles that are confronting the AI community.

It takes a village to solve these riddles.

Isolated attempts to figure out the answers are likely to be insufficient and unable to scale.

Recall that the panel topic was entitled as collaboration for the safety of autonomous vehicles. The watchword there is collaboration.

Ultimately, all stakeholders will need to weigh-in on these matters, and the sooner that we make the riddles known, hopefully, the sooner and more elegantly the answers will emerge.

CHAPTER 8
SPURRING FINANCIAL LITERACY VIA
AI SELF-DRIVING CARS

CHAPTER 8

SPURRING FINANCIAL LITERACY VIA AI SELF-DRIVING CARS

It is said that many Americans are so busy trying to earn money that they don't have time to think about how to best leverage and save money.

This seemingly puzzling statement highlights that we are all on a frantic and mind-numbing treadmill of trying to earn income, yet we oftentimes don't realize that due to financial illiteracy there's a lot of dough being left on the table or going out the door imprudently.

Bad money management and rampant lack of personal financial literacy is the watchword about how Americans deal with their finances.

Stats show that nearly half of all Americans have insufficient cash to cover an unexpected out-of-pocket expense of just $400, and dismally there are about one-third of Americans that have no retirement savings set aside for their future.

Millennials are perhaps in the worst boat as they are often saddled with onerous student debt, amounting to over $1.5 trillion total student debt across the United States and weighing down on 45 million Americans.

Repeated calls are being made to add financial literacy courses into the schools.

Some say that personal finance classes ought to be offered, or perhaps required, for all high schoolers, while others believe that financial awareness should get underway sooner, such as starting in elementary school and then progressing to more sophisticated financial wizardry in the later grades.

Given that the school schedules are already jam-packed with core subjects, the odds of having widespread financial literacy classes get sandwiched into the everyday curriculum is sadly unlikely.

There you have it, there's just no time and no availability to help Americans climb-up the financial awareness ladder, and therefore the leaking faucet of money going down the drain needlessly is bound to continue.

But, please, don't give up hope.

Here's an interesting point to consider: *The advent of true self-driving cars is likely to enable Americans to become financially savvy and take much better care of their personal finances.*

Say what?

Let's unpack the matter and see.

The Levels Of Self-Driving Cars

It is important to clarify what I mean when referring to true self-driving cars.

True self-driving cars are ones that the AI drives the car entirely on its own and there isn't any human assistance during the driving task.

These driverless vehicles are considered a Level 4 and Level 5, while a car that requires a human driver to co-share the driving effort is usually considered at a Level 2 or Level 3. The cars that co-share the driving task are described as being semi-autonomous, and typically contain a variety of automated add-on's that are referred to as ADAS (Advanced Driver-Assistance Systems).

There is not yet a true self-driving car at Level 5, which we don't yet even know if this will be possible to achieve, and nor how long it will take to get there.

Meanwhile, the Level 4 efforts are gradually trying to get some traction by undergoing very narrow and selective public roadway trials, though there is controversy over whether this testing should be allowed per se (we are all life-or-death guinea pigs in an experiment taking place on our highways and byways, some point out).

Since semi-autonomous cars require a human driver, the adoption of those types of cars won't be markedly different than driving conventional vehicles, so there's not much new per se to cover about them on this topic (though, as you'll see in a moment, the points next made are generally applicable).

For semi-autonomous cars, it is important that the public be forewarned about a disturbing aspect that's been arising lately, namely that in spite of those human drivers that keep posting videos of themselves falling asleep at the wheel of a Level 2 or Level 3 car, we all need to avoid being misled into believing that the driver can take away their attention from the driving task while driving a semi-autonomous car.

You are the responsible party for the driving actions of the vehicle, regardless of how much automation might be tossed into a Level 2 or Level 3.

Self-Driving Cars And Financial Literacy Boon

For Level 4 and Level 5 true self-driving vehicles, there won't be a human driver involved in the driving task.

All occupants will be passengers.

The AI is doing the driving.

That seems pretty cool, but you might be scratching your head about how this relates to financial literacy among Americans.

First, since humans won't need to drive, this frees up the existing 70 billion hours of driving time that Americans do each year.

When you are driving a car, your attention is presumably riveted on the act of driving and you can't really do much of anything else (sure, I realize that some people put on their make-up or shave their beard, and do other ill-advised tasks while driving, but on-the-main people are generally focused on the driving chore while at the wheel).

People that used to drive their cars will no longer need to drive and instead will become passengers.

How is all of this newly found time as a passenger going to be used?

There are going to be LED displays mounted on the interior of self-driving cars that can be used to do Facetime-like interactive video, allowing you to confer during your commute with fellow workers already at the office, or perhaps could be used to discuss with your children at home what they are going to do at school that day.

Internet access while inside self-driving cars will be blazingly fast as spurred by the adoption of 5G and other high-def high-speed electronic communications.

The interior of self-driving cars is more malleable due to the removal of the driving controls since there's no need to have a steering wheel and no pedals on the floor. Various concept designs suggest that there will be swivel chairs for seating and possibly a small table amidst the seats.

Voila, this provides a grand convergence of time, availability, and the right working space and equipment to boost the financial literacy of those that are riding inside true self-driving cars.

Here's how:

- **Online video courses about financial literacy.** While you are commuting to work or heading home at night, it will be easy to bring up a financial literacy course on the interior screens and learn what you need to know about personal finances. Sit back, relax, let the AI do the driving while you watch videos about how to better earn and save your money.

- **Interactive training about financial literacy.** Rather than somewhat passively watching videos, the Facetime-like capability inside the driverless car would enable you to take interactive classes. You could ask the remote instructor questions and be sifting through your own personal finances while taking such a course.

- **Access to your financial institutions**. You can readily do your online banking while traveling in a driverless car. Connect with your financial institution via the Internet, just as you might do at home, and carry out any needed financial transactions. No need to wait until you get home and try to deal with banking stuff at night, plus this way you can spend more time with the kids and aiding them on their evening time homework assignments.

- **Interactive online access to financial advisors.** Using the Skype-like capabilities of a self-driving car, you can undertake interactive sessions with your financial advisors. This is handy too since you are inside a private place that allows you to speak freely without being overheard, which can be hard to find during the day if you are at work.

- **AI-based financial "robots" and FinTech.** There's gradually emerging a lot of AI-based financial systems, often referred to as FinTech, and you'll be able to make use of those "online robot" systems while riding in a driverless car. Thus, rather than speaking with a human financial advisor via your remote access, the AI-based financial advisor might be a capability already on-board the computer system of the driverless car or be accessed via the cloud.

- **Dual-use of human financial advisors and AI-based ones.** An interesting twist that some are envisioning is that you might have an AI-based financial advisor that serves as your ally while you are carrying on discussions with say a stockbroker or other financial salesperson. The AI is on your side and uses Natural Language Processing (NLP) to figure out whether you are getting solid financial advice or being sold on a piece of swampland.

- **Financial adviser as a ride-a-long.** Some financial firms are likely to provide their financial advisors on a ride-a-long basis. These specialty riders will spend their day sitting inside driverless cars, being available to chat with a passenger about their financial aspects. I realize this seems odd and maybe a bit creepy, yet if a bank or similar institution was offering free rides in driverless cars and the deal was that you had a financial advisor that went along too, would you take them up on the offer? Some certainly will.

- **Getting you to a financial institution.** Keep in mind that a self-driving car is still a car, which means that it can also be used as a simple form of transport and get you to the nearest ATM or a local banking branch. For people that today are mobility disadvantaged, they can't readily make such a journey, while via an AI self-driving car they are likely to be able to do so (it's considered a mobility-for-all innovation).

- **Kids and financial literacy.** The aforementioned points are self-driving car elements that are primarily aimed at adults, but there are going to be kids using driverless cars too, doing so as they go to school and when they seek to participate in extracurricular activities and need a lift. Short video snippets about financial literacy might be sensible to showcase while the kids are otherwise daydreaming inside a driverless car.

- **Financial literacy club that meets in-car.** Suppose that one morning per week you agree to be in a financial literacy club that meets inside a self-driving car while on the journey to downtown for going to work. Assuming you are comfortable discussing your finances with these other people, this is a handy way to use the commute time.

One nice aspect of these in-car activities is that there isn't a human driver that can overhear your private discussions or interrupt your financial literacy sessions.

Of course, there might be other strangers inside a driverless car that you are ridesharing, and so you'd need to be cautious about undertaking any private financial activity in their presence.

Caveats About Financial Activity

We are all sensitive about our personal finances and thus the idea of doing any financial activity while inside a driverless car is going to raise potential qualms.

If you own a self-driving car, you might feel better that the effort while inside is a private matter, though you might also be lending out your driverless car onto a ridesharing network, doing so to allow it to make money while you are at work during the day or sleeping at night.

Thus, it will be crucial to not somehow leave anything behind inside the self-driving car that could be then picked-up or seen by someone else that ends up in the driverless car.

When using a driverless car that's available via a ridesharing network, you might rightfully be worried that the owner of the self-driving car has rigged the interior or the online access systems to record what you do, or otherwise snoop on you.

Equally bad is that other riders might try to do the same thing, essentially placing something into a self-driving car after they've gotten a lift and use that device to record or snoop on what you do while riding in that particular self-driving car.

In theory, if a human driver was driving a ridesharing car, say an Uber or Lyft driver, they would notice if a passenger left behind a snooping device. In that case of AI self-driving cars, this might not be so easily ascertained, though the odds are that driverless cars will eventually have the means to try and figure out if someone has left something in the vehicle.

Another factor is cybersecurity.

Will the owner of a driverless car have put in place sufficient cybersecurity protections to allow you to securely do your financial banking and other access while on a journey?

There are bound to be cyber hackers that are trying to break into AI self-driving cars overall, using remote hacking tools.

Besides wishing to take over the AI self-driving car, they might want to use their criminal access to snoop on riders.

Conclusion

Some of the driverless car fleet owners might purposely market their self-driving cars for use in these financial literacy ways.

As such, the fleet might contain special privacy features and extra cybersecurity precautions, along with pre-established financial access and an easy means to do so.

Imagine an automaker that does a deal with a financial institution and agrees to co-produce and co-market driverless cars for boosting the financial literacy of riders.

This makes sense for the financial institution as they are always seeking a competitive edge to reach their markets, and meanwhile, the automakers will eventually need to convince people to ride their driverless cars rather than the driverless cars of a competitor.

It will likely be unsavory for one automaker to try and advertise that their self-driving car is safer than another brand, which would bring up the safety issue and possibly turn-off people from wanting to ride in driverless cars altogether.

In what other ways could an automaker or fleet owner then differentiate their driverless cars?

One approach would be by providing a financial literacy capability for passengers.

There is though one big distractor that could undermine the hope of having people gain financial literacy while inside a driverless car.

Cat videos.

Yes, people might decide that they'd rather watch cat videos during their time inside a self-driving car.

Maybe we can tie together cat videos with financial literacy sessions, a goldmine of an idea.

CHAPTER 9
GM CRUISE MINIVAN
AND
AI SELF-DRIVING CARS

CHAPTER 9

GM CRUISE MINIVAN
AND AI SELF-DRIVING CARS

At a grand spectacle in San Francisco last night, the GM-backed Cruise that aims to bring forth autonomous vehicles with true self-driving capabilities had an unveiling of their newest creation (said to have been devised via engineers from GM, Cruise, and Honda).

It has been christened as the Origin.

Looking akin to a minivan, the Origin is a boxy vehicle touted as being an EV that is destined for ride-sharing purposes, and was feted as a solution that is self-driven, all-electric, and shared.

The evening event was primarily devoted to the hardware side of things, eschewing any in-depth indication about advances on the AI and software side (actually, there weren't many specific details on the hardware either, though an actual vehicle was presented and made available to touch and see).

Alas, there were no details about the battery range, nor what kinds of speeds are intended, nor maneuverability characteristics, and most importantly for those focused on self-driving tech there wasn't a detailed indication about the sensors, sensor types and what their capabilities consist of.

You might rate this as an unveiling with perhaps one eye closed.

That being said, please don't misunderstand that somehow showcasing the nature of an intended self-driving car vehicle and not covering all the rest is necessarily an undue affair.

We are going to need a physical car or some kind of vehicle for any kind of self-driving transport, so the hardware in terms of the overall shape and nature of the automobile is indeed important.

It is helpful to the industry and the advancement of self-driving cars to have the automakers strut their stuff in terms of what they envision true self-driving vehicles are going to be like.

Some immediately expressed that the Origin seemed to resemble the VW Cedric concept self-driving van that was unveiled in 2017 at the Geneva Motor Show.

Well, come to think of it, there is such a resemblance, along with similarities to many other concept self-driving vehicle box-designs that have been floated over the years.

Odd coincidence?

Nope.

The point is that we are gradually witnessing a coalescing toward one kind of specialty of a self-driving car, essentially a pod on wheels.

Does this mean that all self-driving cars are destined to be boxy pods?

No.

Let me say that again, no.

It just means that of the various styles and designs for self-driving cars, one that is going to gain traction is the pod.

Indeed, for the cynics that were quick to challenge the pod-like design of the Origin, you've got to keep in mind that customarily a vehicle is purpose-devised (structured and shaped for a specific intended purpose or use case).

If you want a vehicle to serve a particular market or purpose, it makes sense to design the vehicle accordingly.

Sports cars look like sports cars, while minivans look like minivans, and you can't carp about the matter.

Of course, you could try to criticize if someone was aiming at sports cars though the market needed minivans, and likewise, you could complain if an automaker pursued minivans when instead the market really needed sports cars.

In the case of the Origin, since the stated purpose is for ride-sharing, the use of a pod-like design is in keeping with that purpose.

This does not preclude other kinds of self-driving vehicles to also emerge, and nor does it suggest that we will only have self-driving pods on our roadways.

One slightly over-the-top notion though is the suggestion by some that this is a reinventing of what we think a car is.

Sorry, a bit of an overreach.

I'd argue that we are still going to have "cars" in terms of genuinely looking cars that are self-driving. In addition, we'll have pods or minivans that are self-driving. We'll have buses that are self-driving. And, I'll blow your mind perhaps by claiming that we'll have sports cars that are self-driving (see my discussion at **the link here**).

The Origin is essentially a shuttle or pod or minivan, whichever vernacular you prefer, and represents one segment of the burgeoning self-driving "car" marketplace.

Now that I've cleared up that aspect, let's get to the brass tacks.

Based on the rather scant reveal, and subject to further elocution once more details are inexorably shared, here are three key ways that the Origin might find itself facing some heartburn.

This is not solely aimed at the Origin, and other pod designs are likely to have similar kinds of both strengths and weaknesses that need to be contended with.

Interior Space Design

Imagine that you could chuck out the window of a conventional car the steering wheel and pedals.

Man, you'd have a great opportunity to rethink the design of the interior space.

There's no need to have a seat devoted to a human driver.

You can put the seats wherever you want.

One of the most popular concept designs consists of swivel seats, allowing passengers to swivel and face each other, or face toward the front, or face toward the back, or face toward the sides and look out the windows in whatever direction they prefer.

Furthermore, the swivel seats allow for a potential working arrangement, whereby you might place a small table at the center of the vehicle. Passengers could face each other, carry on a dialogue, and use the table for getting their joint efforts undertaken.

That's not the Origin.

Another concept design consists of having seats that are luxurious and recline.

In fact, the reclining might be so extensive that you can pretty much lay down and sleep while inside the self-driving vehicle. For those that take long commutes to work, it could be a godsend that you'd now be able to catch some snoozing, so you'll be fresh and ready to get to work once you arrive at the office.

That's not the Origin.

For the Origin, the designers apparently decided that this pod would be for people on-the-go that are going to leap into the minivan, be whisked to their destination, and then jump out once they get there.

No sleeping (presumably), no working (at least not in the swivel seat manner), all of which makes sense to not do if you are on a quick-ride shuttle.

Here's how the interior is shaped.

There are two benches, essentially, each bench facing the other, akin to if you sat in a shuttle.

One bench faces toward the back, the other faces toward the front.

Each bench consists of three seating positions, though it is really more like two people and maybe you could jam in-between them a child or someone rather slim in stature.

The seating capacity is comfortably for four people, and the stated max is six people, though as I say you'd be somewhat hard-pressed with six strangers sitting in there (they'd get to know each, a bit more so than they might prefer, if you know what I mean).

The seats appear to be unadorned, meaning that it has that straight-backed feel as per a shuttle, unlike bucket seats that you'd find inside an everyday car.

Generally, you would not likely wish to sit in such seats for any lengthy trip, and thus once again reinforces the design notion that this is a shuttle or pod for short hops along with a quick entry and exit.

Under each seat is a small space for passengers to place some belongings, similar somewhat to how you might put items under your seat while in an airplane, though in this pod you have ready access to the area directly underneath your own seat.

Here are a few heartburn aspects of the interior space design that I predict will arise once the Origin is used in real-world settings:

- Placing items under the seat

Riders are going to forget that they placed something under their seat and in their hasty exit from the Origin.

Meanwhile, presumably, the Origin scoots along to whatever its next destination is.

The passenger that left their item might later realize they mistakenly did so and will try to access the ride-sharing network to see if they can get that Origin to come back to them.

That's a logistic nightmare.

Meanwhile, perhaps someone else has already taken the item, figuring that it's a dog-eat-dog world of winners are keepers and losers are weepers.

You might normally have had a chance that a human driver would realize a passenger left an item, and perhaps keep it secure or report it to HQ but recall that there's no human driver involved.

If there are cameras pointed inward in the Origin, which there might well be, and its something that many self-driving vehicles are going to include, the ride-sharing system could potentially take a peek to see if the item is still there, though this raises other privacy issues and isn't a slam dunk solution.

They might put sensors on the floor under the seats, trying to detect the presence of objects, and then alert a passenger as they get up to leave, though this too has a slew of complications.

Anyway, as you can see, a driverless shuttle with the nicety of under-the-seat storage has its tradeoffs.

- Storage at the front and rear

Perhaps even more vexing is the storage compartments that are apparently at the front and rear of the Origin.

It's a good idea to allow people to place their bulky items in such storage compartments, aiming to prevent clutter inside where the passengers are sitting, but unfortunately this is a whole can of worms.

Here's why.

Assume that you are in a rush and want to use an Origin to get a few blocks down the street in your downtown area.

An Origin comes up to the curb, you get in and buckle-up.

The Origin goes about a half-block and picks up the next passenger.

This person has two bags of groceries and wants to place them into the front compartment. They fumble with the compartment and feebly place their bags into it. Oops, one bag tears and the contents spill. The person tries to pick them up and shove them into the other bag.

All of this is taking time.

You are seated in the Origin, wanting to get a few blocks down the street, and your ride is suddenly going to take ten times longer than you estimated.

If there was a human driver, perhaps the driver would help the person load the grocery bags into the trunk and having done so zillions of times the driver is very adept and quick at doing so.

Again, there's no human driver and so the passengers are on their own.

Any self-driving shuttle or pod that allows for compartment space is going to ultimately have to deal with these kinds of issues.

Do you restrict that no one can use the compartments?

It's complicated.

The Same Experience Every Time Is Not Realistic

It was indicated at the unveiling that the Origin will not be a car that you can buy.

Instead, it will be presumably owned by the automaker and deployed as a fleet of self-driving cars, exclusively used for ride-sharing purposes.

That's fine if that's the market position they wish to take.

As I've stated repeatedly, I believe that there will nonetheless also be a market for private ownership of self-driving cars, though I'm a bit of a contrarian since many pundits claim that self-driving cars will only be owned by large firms and used solely as ride-sharing fleets (for my explanation about why private ownership is also viable, see **the link here**).

In any case, the beef that I have about the matter is the claim that supposedly every time you ride in an Origin the experience will be the same every time.

This was explained by the example of getting into an Uber or Lyft today and being knocked over by the smell of Doritos and Mountain Dew, or the biting odor of over-scented Pine-Sol, all of which presumably occur because of a human driver that's either obnoxious or oblivious to the stench inside their ride-sharing car.

In theory, take out the human driver, and you won't have any Doritos and no Mountain Dew.

But, wait, think about that.

You have passengers.

Joe gets into the Origin and has a liverwurst sandwich.

Jane also gets into the Origin and has a raw onion that she loves to eat just like one would eat an apple.

Sam also boards the Origin and he's got a large bag of Doritos Nacho Cheese tortilla chips and his trusty Big Gulp of Mountain Dew.

They have quite a fun time during their ride, and part of Joe's liverwurst sandwich ends-up on the floor, while Sam accidentally spills his Mountain Dew onto the seat, and Jane leaves onion peels all over the place.

Upon reaching their destination, out they go.

You were waiting for the Origin and happily step into it.

Yikes, you can barely breath!

As I've repeatedly stated, a looming problem for the self-driving car ride-sharing era will be the stench fest that is going to arise.

This could be ten times worse than when you have a human driver since the human driver is likely to notice odors or at least do something about odors once they realize that customers are upset.

There's no human driver to clean things up or try to deal with foul odors.

Passengers are free to do whatever they like.

Sure, you might say that the fleet owner needs to ensure that the inside is clean and odor-free.

But, how do you do that for each and every ride?

You can't have your self-driving vehicle continually coming to the home base to get cleaned upon each ride given, it just doesn't make any viable sense.

So, for clarity, a self-driving car that's being used for ride-sharing is not a guarantee of the same experience every time, other than for the driving aspects and the nature of the vehicle (assuming that a fleet is only using one and only one type of vehicle), but not for the nature of the interior and aspects such as odors, cleanliness, etc.

Sensor Innovations

A new sensor was showcased at the unveiling of the Origin.

No specifications were provided, but it appeared to be a sensor that is intended to sit at the exterior corners of the vehicle and pivots back-and-forth on its mounting as though scanning what is in front of the sensor.

This was likened to an owl that moves its head.

Or, akin to how humans move their heads, scanning back-and-forth to survey the driving scene and gauge what's up ahead and to their sides.

The analogy to animals and humans seems compelling.

Sure, if via Darwin's theory we and animals evolved to move our heads back-and-forth, doing so to try and observe both friend and foe, it must make sense to do the same thing in a car.

We'll see.

Anytime that you have a sensory device that relies on physical movement, you are asking for trouble.

The device is likely to wear out or breakdown as a result of the ongoing and presumably continuous movement.

If you rightfully assume that ride-sharing self-driving cars are going to be active 24x7, which makes sense to get your monies worth, other than brief windows of time for maintenance and upkeep, this means those pivoting sensors are going to be on-the-go a lot.

Let's hope the failure rate is really low.

That's partially why too there has been a movement for LIDAR, another type of sensor often used on self-driving cars, involving reducing the number and nature of the moving parts.

Setting aside that concern, another involves whether the pivoting scanner will be looking in the right direction at the right moment in time.

We'll go back to the human analogy.

You look to your left, the coast is clear, you look to your right, and start to make your left turn. Oops, in the moment that you checked the right side, a bicyclist suddenly appeared to your left. Bam, you ram into the bicyclist.

The question is how fast the sensors pivot and whether the pivoting potentially opens any untimely gaps of not spotting what's going on.

There's also the whole aspect of sensor fusion too.

How is the pivoting sensor stitching together the data collected at each stance of the pivot?

Does the pivoting sensor on the left side of the vehicle get mated with the pivoting sensor on the right side of the vehicle, crafting a cohesive whole?

I'm certainly in favor of new kinds of sensors for self-driving cars and have argued vehemently that the more sensors the better, which is contrary to the views of some pundits, though I've also said that not all sensors are ready for prime time and it's important to make sure that the sensors perform a needed function, each providing added value, and collectively working on a unified basis.

Time will tell.

Conclusion

Kudos to GM/Cruise for their willingness to showcase their latest approach to a self-driving car.

Some self-driving tech is being added to conventional cars, such as Waymo's efforts with the Chrysler Pacifica, while in other cases an entirely new vehicle is being made to support self-driving.

There are tradeoffs whichever way you go.

At least we know this, the more that the automakers bring forth their efforts, the sooner that the nature of self-driving cars will evolve and mature.

You might say it's the origin of a new species.

CHAPTER 10

CAR OFF CLIFF LESSONS

AND

AI SELF-DRIVING CARS

CHAPTER 10

CAR OFF CLIFF LESSONS

AND

AI SELF-DRIVING CARS

You are on a mountain road that overlooks the ocean, driving along at 55 miles per hour and enjoying the scenic view.

Up ahead is a tight curve.

The cars coming in the other direction are closely hugging the mountain, fortunately, since they would otherwise potentially veer into your lane.

If you had to escape a head-on collision, there's no option to your right because it is simply a sheer cliff that descends to the rippling sea.

All of a sudden, you see a car that is not going to make the curve and it rockets past you, right in front of your eyes, passing across your lane, and heads to the edge of the cliff in a blur.

To your utter shock, the car pitches off the embankment of the cliff, becoming momentarily airborne, and flies out beyond the cliff.

OMG, you can't believe your eyes.

In the few split seconds that this all plays out, you are meanwhile still zipping along at 55 mph, passing the point at which the car lunged off the cliff, and you can scarcely believe what you just saw happen.

Did you dream it?

Were you delirious after hours of driving?

Your mind is numb.

You try to recall what the driver looked like, but it happened so fast and your viewpoint was so limited that you can't remember even seeing the driver.

Nor did you notice any passengers, though there might have been some, but your memory is cloudy.

You assume that the car plunged down the side of the cliff and landed on the beach or in the ocean below and so you immediately begin to think about calling for the police and emergency rescue.

Indeed, you make that call and the authorities show-up around twenty minutes later (it's a rather remote location in San Mateo County, California and thus took a while for the sheriff and rescue teams to arrive).

And what did the authorities find?

Nothing.

Absolutely nothing.

No car.

No injured people, no deceased bodies.

And yet, despite there being no physical evidence to support the assertion that a car did what you claimed it did, nonetheless an all-out search is undertaken, doing so via boats in the water, helicopters flying overhead, and scouring the ground at the base of the cliff takes place.

Nada.

Was it all a dream, a nightmarish dream?

If so, you weren't the only one that "dreamed" it.

Turns out that another driver happened to catch the flying car on their dashcam.

The video clip has since been posted on the web and been shown repeatedly on various news accounts about the incident.

The mystery remains, namely, what happened to the car and its occupants?

Nobody knows.

Exacerbating the mystery is that the short video clip only shows the car flying into the air.

After the flight, there's no indication of what happened next.

By the law of physics, you would certainly assume that after the car flew briefly, it must have turned downward toward the earth and plunged to its doom.

Yet, there's no car anywhere on the cliff, nor at the bottom, nor that can be found on or in the water.

Suppose somehow the car landed in a spot that cannot be readily found or seen.

At least there would seem to be a chance that the occupants might have lived and then made their way out of the wreck, climbing up to the coast highway to seek medical assistance.

As far as we know, that didn't happen either.

Could the occupants that possibly lived be wandering around aimlessly, maybe semi-conscious and have incurred head injuries that caused them to lose their minds and be truly lost?

Again, if they are alive, no one seems to know.

In terms of the car, you would think that it must have gotten mangled and bounced and slid across the side of the cliff, in which case there would be debris, including smashed parts from the car and maybe tire remnants.

Well, there was some debris later discovered, but the authorities aren't sure that it had to do with this incident and apparently the finding didn't shed any light on the matter.

If you watch the video, and since it doesn't show what occurred after the car went airborne, it allows wild speculation about other possibilities.

Maybe the car perchance landed on a dirt pad position near the top of the cliff, and the driver was able to maneuver the car back onto the highway, doing so before the authorities showed-up about a half-hour after the incident took place.

It's a clever idea, and a cheerful and a rather optimistic glass-is-half-full perspective, but seemingly the rough geography itself does not seem to support such a theory.

Plus, with all the news coverage, don't you think that the driver by now would have come forward to tell their tale?

Imagine how much fame they could get, perhaps a book deal, and eventually a movie made.

The counterargument is that perhaps the driver did survive and turns out was a wanted criminal, escaping the law, and doesn't want to come forward for fear of getting caught on some other beef.

Wow, that's a reach.

Another point made is that perhaps the video itself is faked.

Using so-called deep fake AI technology, such a video could be made, though some "experts" say that it is unlikely to be a deep fake since you would need presumably thousands of instances of cars going off cliffs to make use of Machine Learning (ML) or Deep Learning (DL) to craft such a video (actually, this isn't quite correct, but anyway I won't go into it herein, see my postings **about one-shot ML/DL**).

Of course, other means of video editing could readily produce a faked video of this sort.

Furthermore, realize that the video only shows the car going airborne, and it does not show it falling or landing, thus, the fakery would be relatively easier to pull off.

The problem with trying to claim that the video is fake consists of the aspect that another eyewitness also reported the incident.

So, you've got a video and the video maker that serve as an eyewitness, and a separate person that was driving on the road at the same time that also serves as a witness to the incident.

I suppose you could say it is a concocted conspiracy or a grand hoax.

Perhaps the witnesses are all in on the cahoots.

Maybe, seems doubtful.

Why would they undertake such a ploy?

Sure, there are lots of YouTube videos that were staged, doing so to get views, but in this case, the conspirators would likely face some pretty stiff fines and maybe even jail time, since they caused quite a ruckus and forced the authorities to expend a lot of time and attention to the matter.

Perhaps the car had no occupants at all, and it was rigged to go off the cliff.

If so, how do you explain the utter disappearance of the car, which would have to been recovered and entirely removed within the brief half-hour before the authorities arrived (unless some say, it was staged long ago and made to seem like it just happened now)?

For those of you that enjoy Reddit, the theories posted there are at times hilarious, though if the incident did occur, perhaps we ought not to be making a joke out of it.

One theory (or wisecrack) is that it was another venture by SpaceX and the car is somewhere now in outer space (this is a clever head nod to the fact that Elon Musk launched a Tesla into outer space).

Yet another theory is that this is a Banksy-like performance art project, seemingly a bit macabre one.

In any case, you can study the video just like the analyses that have been done about the infamous Zapruder film of JFK getting shot, which became for some the most important 26-seconds of film history ever and try to figure out what happened.

Upon mulling over the incident of the mystery outcome of the car that went off the cliff, it turns out that there might be some handy lessons to be gleaned.

Here's an interesting notion: *Can the disappearing car that went off the edge of a cliff provide any insights for the advent of true self-driving cars?*

Decidedly so.

Let's unpack the matter and see.

The Levels Of Self-Driving Cars

It is important to clarify what I mean when referring to true self-driving cars.

True self-driving cars are ones that the AI drives the car entirely on its own and there isn't any human assistance during the driving task.

These driverless vehicles are considered a Level 4 and Level 5, while a car that requires a human driver to co-share the driving effort is usually considered at a Level 2 or Level 3. The cars that co-share the driving task are described as being semi-autonomous, and typically contain a variety of automated add-on's that are referred to as ADAS (Advanced Driver-Assistance Systems).

There is not yet a true self-driving car at Level 5, which we don't yet even know if this will be possible to achieve, and nor how long it will take to get there.

Meanwhile, the Level 4 efforts are gradually trying to get some traction by undergoing very narrow and selective public roadway trials, though there is controversy over whether this testing should be allowed per se (we are all life-or-death guinea pigs in an experiment taking place on our highways and byways, some point out).

Since semi-autonomous cars require a human driver, the adoption of those types of cars won't be markedly different than driving conventional vehicles, so there's not much new per se to cover about them on this topic (though, as you'll see in a moment, the points next made are generally applicable).

For semi-autonomous cars, it is important that the public be forewarned about a disturbing aspect that's been arising lately, namely that in spite of those human drivers that keep posting videos of themselves falling asleep at the wheel of a Level 2 or Level 3 car, we all need to avoid being misled into believing that the driver can take away their attention from the driving task while driving a semi-autonomous car.

You are the responsible party for the driving actions of the vehicle, regardless of how much automation might be tossed into a Level 2 or Level 3.

Self-Driving Cars And Car Mishaps

For Level 4 and Level 5 true self-driving vehicles, there won't be a human driver involved in the driving task.

All occupants will be passengers.

The AI is doing the driving.

Inside a true self-driving car, there are these possibilities in terms of occupants:
- No human passengers
- One human passenger
- Two or more human passengers

Notably, in the first use case, the notion that a car can be on our roadways and traveling around and yet not have any humans inside it defies today's world of the need for at least one human to be present, namely the driver.

Why would a self-driving car be on a journey and not have any human occupants?

That's easy, there are going to be a lot of self-driving cars roaming and awaiting being requested for a human trip, and as I've forewarned we might, unfortunately, end up with a lot of the time seeing completely empty self-driving cars wandering on our roadways.

In addition, self-driving cars are undoubtedly going to be used for delivery purposes, thus there might be packages or other items inside the car or perhaps in the trunk, but nonetheless, no human rider will be present.

This brings us to the first intriguing lesson about the mystery of the car that went off a cliff and disappeared.

Suppose a true self-driving car is roaming or on a delivery errand, doing so without any human occupants, and it regrettably goes awry.

By going awry, I'm referring to the possibility that the self-driving car might suddenly have a flat tire or maybe hits a couch that unexpectedly fell from a truck ahead of it.

In such cases, the self-driving car might become disabled or confounded.

For the instance of being disabled, hopefully, the AI and on-board processors will be intact enough to guide the damaged vehicle to the side of the road or bring the car to some other relatively safe position (referred to as a Minimal Risk Condition or MRC in industry parlance).

There's no guarantee that the AI will be able to do so.

It all depends on the severity and extent of the damage done to the vehicle and it's on-board AI systems.

Furthermore, there's also a chance that the AI system itself might end-up having issues, which though there are likely various system redundancy provisions, and hopefully a fault-tolerant capability, there is still a possible chance of the AI going astray.

I mention this aspect since there are many pundits that keep asserting that AI self-driving cars can do no wrong and will always work perfectly.

This is one of those falsehoods that keeps getting repeated.

When I debunk the zero incidents claimants, I usually get a pushback from them on the basis that they say that the odds of such a calamity facing the AI self-driving car is lower than it would be of human drivers (for more on relative risks of self-driving cars, see **this link here**).

Though this has yet to be proven that self-driving cars will be safer than human-driven cars, let's go ahead and concede that it might well be less chancy than human driver instances, but this is certainly not, therefore, a proof or concession that it will be a zero chance altogether.

In other words, there is still a non-zero chance, even for a true self-driving car.

It might be a smaller risk than the human driver foibles, but don't fall into the mental trap that it ergo must be a zero chance.

Why does this matter?

Suppose a true self-driving car is driving on a mountainous road, doing so in a place or region that has spotty or no electronic communications capabilities, such as being on the coast highway in the middle of California.

For whatever reason, the AI of the self-driving car goes afoul, and the vehicle inadequately curves around the bend of the road.

The self-driving car crosses in front of other oncoming cars, barely missing hitting them, and rockets off the edge of the cliff.

It lands somewhere down below.

If there was no one to witness the incident, how would anyone know that the self-driving car is now sitting at the bottom of the cliff and wrecked beyond use?

No one would know.

Presumably, at some point, the self-driving car on its journey would have entered back into an area or zone that did have electronic communications available, and presumably, it would have checked-in with whatever networking system dispatched the driverless car.

After not checking in, the networking system would deduce that something has gone amiss.

At that point, whomever owns the driverless car, or its fleet manager would need to be alerted and try to figure out where the heck the AI self-driving car is.

A self-driving car has fallen down, and it can't get up, one might say.

Realize too that there were no humans inside the driverless car, in this use case, and so there's no chance of a human occupant that might crawl out of the wreckage and seek help (which they would also let the world know about the incident and where the driverless car sits).

In short, the driverless car might seemingly disappear from earth.

Now, I'm not suggesting it got swallowed up whole or that it was beamed up by aliens from another planet.

I'm just saying that it could happen that a true self-driving car could end up in a ditch or someplace and no one would know where it is.

That being said, there are some that believe we ought to require self-driving cars to house a beacon that would automatically activate and allow therefore to trace and find a lost driverless car.

There are Event Data Recorders (EDRs), though they don't necessarily act as a beacon and are oftentimes more so just a hardened black box that contains the last few moments of the selected status of the vehicle prior to it becoming disabled.

I willingly agree that the odds of a true self-driving car being entirely out-of0contact is going to be somewhat slim, though as more and more driverless cars become commonplace, they will likely be giving driving tasks that take them to remote parts of the country.

And, there would need to be a grand convergence of no available electronic communication that becomes coupled with the odds of having the AI self-driving car going awry, all of which will hopefully be low odds, yet nonetheless non-zero odds.

When People Matter

Let's take a quick look at some other similar use cases.

Suppose the same thing happens in the circumstance that there are human passengers?

In one sense, it's no different than if the car was a conventional car and being driven by a human.

Since the self-driving car has lots of sensors, including cameras, radar, ultrasonic, possibly LIDAR, would that change things?

Not really, other than it might provide added information about what happened prior to the incident, though that's not necessarily so, as it depends upon how the data is being stored on-board the driverless car.

One potential "plus" about having self-driving cars on our roadways would be that other driverless cars that witnessed the incident would likely have tons of data about what happened.

Thus, rather than relying upon someone perchance having a dashcam, in a world of self-driving cars there is going to be a plethora of sensory data being collected in real-time of every place that the driverless cars go and of what they see and detect.

That comes with an ugly side to it too.

As I've exhorted repeatedly, we are heading toward an era of privacy invasion, during which driverless cars will be watching everything we do, and the possibility of someone opting to stitch together such data and chart our daily lives is a real concern.

Well, all of this provides food for thought, prompted by the car that disappeared off a cliff.

Sorry to say, the mystery still exists and so far, no amount of human ingenuity and nor AI has figured out where the darned thing is.

Lance B. Eliot

CHAPTER 11

DAUGHTER PRANK AND AI SELF-DRIVING CARS

CHAPTER 11

DAUGHTER PRANK AND
AI SELF-DRIVING CARS

The phrase "Not My Mom" created quite a commotion the other day.

Here's the 411 about it.

A recent news story indicated that a girl in the backseat of a moving car displayed a hand-scrawled sign that said "Not My Mom," doing so while traveling on Highway 99 in Northern California just south of the state capital of Sacramento.

Other motorists that saw the sign were taken aback and instantly became concerned about the welfare of the young girl.

Anxiously, those concerned citizens called 911.

The California Highway Patrol (CHP) immediately dispatched six cruisers, including a K9 unit, aiming to intercept the car.

It was natural to assume that the girl was likely being kidnapped.

As part of the CHP's standard protocol, they were to find the car and undertake what's referred to as a high-risk traffic stop.

Logically, it could be that the child had been kidnapped. Furthermore, the kidnapper was potentially the driver of the vehicle.

And, the driver, being a presumed sordid kidnapper of children, might be armed.

All in all, it was certain to be a dangerous situation for all parties involved.

Turns out, upon performing the high-risk traffic stop, the CHP ascertained that the girl was the daughter of the driver (her now mortified mother) and that the girl was just having some fun.

The mother insisted she did not know that her daughter was holding up the sign.

Since everything seemed to be on the up-and-up, the CHP let the mother and daughter continue on their way.

As an aside, the handcrafted sign actually said this: "Help me, She's not my mom!! Help!!"

Any conscientious person would certainly have been alarmed upon seeing such a sign, and I'd suggest we should be thankful that the motorists opted to call the police.

Believe it or not, there were some critics that suggested the motorists that made the call to the authorities were hasty and should have not done so.

Say what?

Would you have motorists entirely ignore such a sign?

That seems like a sad and perhaps outdated way of thinking, namely don't get involved in matters that aren't of your concern (what happened to see something, say something?).

I would hope that most people would, in fact, be filled with concern upon witnessing such a situation.

I suppose some critics might argue that the concerned motorists should have flagged down the driver or otherwise made an attempt to get the driver to pull over.

That doesn't seem very prudent either.

If the driver was a kidnapper, efforts to notify them about the sign would merely play into their hands and undoubtedly, they would have threatened the girl to put down the sign, along with then continuing the kidnapping effort.

Not a good option.

Seeking instead to outright block or stop the car by yourself would be dangerous and foolhardy.

For a kidnapper, they might purposely evade being stopped and you'd end up with a wild and endangering car chase.

Or, the kidnapper might have a gun and start shooting at you and other motorists.

Some say that it was "obvious" that since there was a woman driving, the woman was most likely her mom.

Please keep in mind that the sign explicitly said the opposite, namely that the driver was not her mom, and the girl holding up the sign was old enough to be able to write the sign and presumably be cognizant of what she was conveying.

It seems reasonable to believe that the sign was true and that the woman driving the car might not be the girl's mother.

Another crazy idea floated was that the motorists ought to have waved at the driver and gotten the female driver to pull over the car.

I ask you whether you would pull over your car on the highway if some other motorist started waving frantically at you and you didn't know what their beef was.

In other words, put yourself into the shoes of the mother, professing to not have known about the sign, and all of a sudden other motorists are making crazy motions toward you.

Once again, not a reasonable notion.

I say that we put to bed the belligerent qualms about what the motorists did.

They did what we, as a society, would hope would be done.

The Underlying Motivations

Switching away from the details of the incident, maybe we might want to consider why the girl crafted the sign and opted to put it on display.

According to reported accounts, the girl thought it would be fun to do.

Was it solely a lark or whimsy?

Some suggest that perhaps the girl might have already had anger toward the mother and decided this might be a means to get back at her mom.

Maybe, maybe not.

In today's age, it could even be a YouTube prompted effort, either that the girl had seen online videos of others playing a similar prank, or that maybe the girl hoped she would gain some YouTube fame by having others videotape her.

Did social media play into this?

We don't know.

It could also have been borne from pure boredom, during which the girl decided to do something that would provoke reactions from other drivers.

Some say that the mother ought to take the full blame in the matter.

Yes, that's right, some indeed make that claim.

Those proponents assert that the mother should have known what her daughter was doing while in the backseat of the car.

How terrible of the mother to not be keeping tabs on her daughter, they argue.

Look, a daughter old enough to care for themselves while sitting in the backseat of a car is not the same as having a baby in a baby seat or a toddler that needs close supervision.

Give me a break that the mother was supposed to be so closely monitoring her daughter's efforts in this instance, and especially tough since the daughter was apparently shielding the sign from the mother and did not in any manner alert or inform the mother of the prank underway.

Get ready for something equally a stretch.

Another basis for blaming the mother is that presumably, the mom had not taught her daughter the difference between right and wrong.
Had the mother done a good job of instructing her child about moral values, the daughter would have known to not pull this kind of a stunt, they contend.

All I can say is that if you are really of the mind that this kind of prank is evidence that a mother has not properly reared her daughter (let alone cast blame on all others that are adults in the life of the daughter), you are living in some kind of make-believe world.

Furthermore, even if the mother had dutifully been giving right versus wrong guidance to the child, it would be farfetched to think that the mother perchance covered the instance of don't hold up a sign that says not my mom.

That being said, one can likely assume that the mother had covered general principles of life and the girl might very well have realized that the prank was inappropriate, but such guidance was presumably overridden on a spur of the moment whim.

It seems unlikely that the daughter realized the full ramifications of her pranking actions.

The daughter probably figured that motorists might honk their horns or wave at her, but one wonders if she truly realized that the police would show up in force and that the matter had an intensely serious and life-threatening potential to it.

Don't get me wrong, I'm not excusing the girl for what she did.

During the proverbial kids-will-be-kid's predicaments of raising children, these kinds of circumstances can arise and luckily, the end results, in this case, was that no one got hurt. Hopefully, the girl comes away with a new lesson in life and does so without being psychology lifelong scarred for what occurred (nor would we want her to simply shrug it off and somehow exaggeratingly start a life of crime).

Here's an interesting aspect to ponder: What do you think the mother told the child after the police let them proceed?

That must have been quite a conversation during the rest of the ride home.

Makes you wonder, how many days of being grounded do you think got assigned?

All of this brings up another interesting topic to ponder: *What lessons can be learned about AI self-driving cars as a result of the "Not My Mom" incident?*

Plenty!

Let's unpack the matter and see.

The Levels Of Self-Driving Cars

It is important to clarify what I mean when referring to true self-driving cars.

True self-driving cars are ones that the AI drives the car entirely on its own and there isn't any human assistance during the driving task.

These driverless vehicles are considered a Level 4 and Level 5, while a car that requires a human driver to co-share the driving effort is usually considered at a Level 2 or Level 3. The cars that co-share the driving task are described as being semi-autonomous, and typically contain a variety of automated add-on's that are referred to as ADAS (Advanced Driver-Assistance Systems).

There is not yet a true self-driving car at Level 5, which we don't yet even know if this will be possible to achieve, and nor how long it will take to get there.

Meanwhile, the Level 4 efforts are gradually trying to get some traction by undergoing very narrow and selective public roadway trials, though there is controversy over whether this testing should be allowed per se (we are all life-or-death guinea pigs in an experiment taking place on our highways and byways, some point out).

Since semi-autonomous cars require a human driver, the adoption of those types of cars won't be markedly different than driving conventional vehicles, so there's not much new per se to cover about them on this topic (though, as you'll see in a moment, the points next made are generally applicable).

For semi-autonomous cars, it is important that the public be forewarned about a disturbing aspect that's been arising lately, namely that in spite of those human drivers that keep posting videos of themselves falling asleep at the wheel of a Level 2 or Level 3 car, we all need to avoid being misled into believing that the driver can take away their attention from the driving task while driving a semi-autonomous car.

You are the responsible party for the driving actions of the vehicle, regardless of how much automation might be tossed into a Level 2 or Level 3.

Self-Driving Cars And Rider Pranks

For Level 4 and Level 5 true self-driving vehicles, there won't be a human driver involved in the driving task.

All occupants will be passengers.

The AI is doing the driving.

This means that a mother that's riding with her daughter in an AI self-driving car will be able to fully devote attention to her loving offspring.

The odds that the daughter could get away with displaying a handwritten sign are pretty slim, though maybe if the sign said "My Mom Is Great" then the mother would allow it to happen.

Seems like this means that we won't need to worry about similar hoaxes in the future.

Case closed.

Whoa, not so fast!

One aspect that as a society we have yet to wrestle with involves having children ride in AI self-driving cars by themselves.

Yes, we are ultimately going to have children without any adult supervision that will be riding around in AI-driven cars.

Your first reaction is likely to be that you'd never let your children ride in an AI self-driving car without having an adult present. The very idea seems foolish and untenable.

Not all parents are going to think that it is such a verboten notion.

Imagine that you are at work and don't have the time to get over to the school to pick-up your son or daughter since you are at the office, which is about an hour away from the child's campus.

After school, your offspring needs to be given a lift to piano practice, just a short 10-minute drive from school.

You don't have any other adult that you know or trust to go pick-up the child.

What do you do?

Send the child an AI self-driving car and have it drive the child over to piano practice.

Problem solved.

I've previously predicted that we are going to end up with a new role in society, the specialist nanny or similar that is a ride-a-long companion and (more importantly) supervisor of children that are riding in a true self-driving car.

Some ride-sharing services that make use of self-driving cars will potentially offer the adult supervisor for an added fee, plus there are likely to be independent services that will hire out such personnel.

Not everyone though will be able to afford the added cost of the ride-a-long adult.

Plus, some would rather take a chance on having their child ride without an adult, versus the off chance that a hired "stranger" adult might otherwise do something untoward while riding in the car with their child.

It's going to be a tough trade-off.

Okay, let's agree that some parents will let their children ride in a true self-driving car all by themselves.

Guess what?

Such a child might handwrite a sign and display it while riding inside the self-driving car.

Of course, saying "Not My Mom" wouldn't make any sense since the mother isn't in the self-driving car.

On the other hand, a clever and mischievous child could write other remarks that suggest something adverse is occurring.

Perhaps something like "Help! Being Kidnapped!!" might be enough to get a reaction from other motorists.

Those motorists might call the police.

If you are wondering how the police are going to stop an AI self-driving car, there are lots of potential ways that as a society we are likely to allow this to occur.

Options include having the police carry some kind of electronic indicator to let the on-board AI know to stop, or perhaps having the authorities contact the fleet owner and have them transmit a special code to the driving system of the vehicle via an OTA (Over-The-Air) electronic capability, etc.

Anyway, the point is that we are once again faced with the potential of children playing a prank while inside a car.

As might be evident, removing the human driver is both a blessing and perhaps in some ways a potential curse.

Without the need for a human driver, we are removing the adult supervision that today is an assumed and required element of riding inside cars.

Today's method of driving involves a human driver that might not be aware of what's happening in the backseat.

The future consists of no human driver in the car and presumably wanton antics by any children that are riding in a driverless car.

Will this lead to anarchy and chaos?

No, for the reasons given next.

More That Meets The Eye

It is anticipated that most driverless cars will include cameras that not only face outward but also ones that face inward.

An inward-facing camera will be handy for many purposes.

Suppose you are riding in a self-driving car to work in the morning. You need to do a Skype-like session with colleagues that are already in the office. Voila, you activate the inward-facing camera, and also the LED display that's inside the driverless car, and you carry on your work activity remotely.

Another use of the inward-facing cameras will be to try and prevent people from trashing the inside of ride-sharing self-driving cars.

Sadly, without a human driver present, the odds are that some people will decide to spray paint graffiti or rip-up the seats of the driverless car.

To reduce the chances of this happening, the inward-facing camera will be used similar to cameras in liquor stores and other retail establishments. You'll always be under the eagle eye of the camera. Even if the camera isn't being manned at all times by some remote operator, the video will be recorded, and you'll be ultimately caught for doing interior damage.

Here's how this applies to the matter of children riding in self-driving cars.

You send a driverless car to pick-up your child at school. Once your child gets into the vehicle, you turn-on remotely the camera. While sitting at your desk at work, you watch your child riding in the driverless car. Furthermore, you chat about how their day is going and then wish them well at piano practice when the driverless car reaches its destination.

In that manner, there is adult supervision.

Don't though rejoice entirely.

Being remote has its disadvantages.

If the child is eating and suddenly starts to choke, there's nothing much you can do. Not being present in the driverless car does have disadvantages.

Though, at least you could talk to the child and try to explain what to do.

You might also be able to alert the police and ask them to rush to the driverless car to help save your child.

And, you could likely remotely instruct the AI to pull over where there might be adults that could extend a hand.

Conclusion

Does this mean that whenever children are in a driverless car there will always be some form of remote adult supervision?

No.

It might be that you don't have the time to watch the child or believe that there's no need to watch the child (especially if they are a teenager or so-called young adult).

In the end, no matter what AI self-driving cars are able to do, it seems like a pretty strong bet that kids will still be kids.

One wonders if the AI of a self-driving car perchance spies a sign in the window of another driverless car that has a child holding up a sign saying "AI Has Me Captive," whether or not the AI of the spotting driverless car will do something to save the child, or instead will loyalty to a fellow (artificial) species override being a tattletale.

Time will tell.

APPENDIX

APPENDIX A
TEACHING WITH THIS MATERIAL

The material in this book can be readily used either as a supplemental to other content for a class, or it can also be used as a core set of textbook material for a specialized class. Classes where this material is most likely used include any classes at the college or university level that want to augment the class by offering thought provoking and educational essays about AI and self-driving cars.

In particular, here are some aspects for class use:

o   Computer Science. Studying AI, autonomous vehicles, etc.

o   Business. Exploring technology and it adoption for business.

o   Sociology. Sociological views on the adoption and advancement of technology.

Specialized classes at the undergraduate and graduate level can also make use of this material.

For each chapter, consider whether you think the chapter provides material relevant to your course topic. There is plenty of opportunity to get the students thinking about the topic and force them to decide whether they agree or disagree with the points offered and positions taken. I would also encourage you to have the students do additional research beyond the chapter material presented (I provide next some suggested assignments they can do).

RESEARCH ASSIGNMENTS ON THESE TOPICS

Your students can find background material on these topics, doing so in various business and technical publications. I list below the top ranked AI related journals. For business publications, I would suggest the usual culprits such as the Harvard Business Review, Forbes, Fortune, WSJ, and the like.

Here are some suggestions of homework or projects that you could assign to students:

a) <u>Assignment for foundational AI research topic</u>: Research and prepare a paper and a presentation on a specific aspect of Deep AI, Machine Learning, ANN, etc. The paper should cite at least 3 reputable sources. Compare and contrast to what has been stated in this book.

b) <u>Assignment for the Self-Driving Car topic</u>: Research and prepare a paper and Self-Driving Cars. Cite at least 3 reputable sources and analyze the characterizations. Compare and contrast to what has been stated in this book.

c) <u>Assignment for a Business topic</u>: Research and prepare a paper and a presentation on businesses and advanced technology. What is hot, and what is not? Cite at least 3 reputable sources. Compare and contrast to the depictions in this book.

d) <u>Assignment to do a Startup:</u> Have the students prepare a paper about how they might startup a business in this realm. They must submit a sound Business Plan for the startup. They could also be asked to present their Business Plan and so should also have a presentation deck to coincide with it.

You can certainly adjust the aforementioned assignments to fit to your particular needs and the class structure. You'll notice that I ask for 3 reputable cited sources for the paper writing based assignments. I usually steer students toward "reputable" publications, since otherwise they will cite some oddball source that has no credentials other than that they happened to write something and post it onto the Internet. You can define "reputable" in whatever way you prefer, for example some faculty think Wikipedia is not reputable while others believe it is reputable and allow students to cite it.

The reason that I usually ask for at least 3 citations is that if the student only does one or two citations they usually settle on whatever they happened to find the fastest. By requiring three citations, it usually seems to force them to look around, explore, and end-up probably finding five or more, and then whittling it down to 3 that they will actually use.

I have not specified the length of their papers, and leave that to you to tell the students what you prefer. For each of those assignments, you could end-up with a short one to two pager, or you could do a dissertation length paper. Base the length on whatever best fits for your class, and the credit amount of the assignment within the context of the other grading metrics you'll be using for the class.

I mention in the assignments that they are to do a paper and prepare a presentation. I usually try to get students to present their work. This is a good practice for what they will do in the business world. Most of the time, they will be required to prepare an analysis and present it. If you don't have the class time or inclination to have the students present, then you can of course cut out the aspect of them putting together a presentation.

If you want to point students toward highly ranked journals in AI, here's a list of the top journals as reported by *various citation counts sources* (this list changes year to year):

- o   Communications of the ACM
- o   Artificial Intelligence
- o   Cognitive Science
- o   IEEE Transactions on Pattern Analysis and Machine Intelligence
- o   Foundations and Trends in Machine Learning
- o   Journal of Memory and Language
- o   Cognitive Psychology
- o   Neural Networks
- o   IEEE Transactions on Neural Networks and Learning Systems
- o   IEEE Intelligent Systems
- o   Knowledge-based Systems

GUIDE TO USING THE CHAPTERS

For each of the chapters, I provide next some various ways to use the chapter material. You can assign the tasks as individual homework assignments, or the tasks can be used with team projects for the class. You can easily layout a series of assignments, such as indicating that the students are to do item "a" below for say Chapter 1, then "b" for the next chapter of the book, and so on.

a) What is the main point of the chapter and describe in your own words the significance of the topic,

b) Identify at least two aspects in the chapter that you agree with, and support your concurrence by providing at least one other outside researched item as support; make sure to explain your basis for disagreeing with the aspects,

c) Identify at least two aspects in the chapter that you disagree with, and support your disagreement by providing at least one other outside researched item as support; make sure to explain your basis for disagreeing with the aspects,

d) Find an aspect that was not covered in the chapter, doing so by conducting outside research, and then explain how that aspect ties into the chapter and what significance it brings to the topic,

e) Interview a specialist in industry about the topic of the chapter, collect from them their thoughts and opinions, and readdress the chapter by citing your source and how they compared and contrasted to the material,

f) Interview a relevant academic professor or researcher in a college or university about the topic of the chapter, collect from them their thoughts and opinions, and readdress the chapter by citing your source and how they compared and contrasted to the material,

g) Try to update a chapter by finding out the latest on the topic, and ascertain whether the issue or topic has now been solved or whether it is still being addressed, explain what you come up with.

The above are all ways in which you can get the students of your class involved in considering the material of a given chapter. You could mix things up by having one of those above assignments per each week, covering the chapters over the course of the semester or quarter.

As a reminder, here are the chapters of the book and you can select whichever chapters you find most valued for your particular class:

<u>Chapter Title</u>

1   Eliot Framework for AI Self-Driving Cars

2   Backup Drivers and AI Self-Driving Cars

3   Teaching Kids about AI Self-Driving Cars

4   Hand-off Problem and AI Self-Driving Cars

5   Racial Bias and AI Self-Driving Cars

6   AI Consciousness and AI Self-Driving Cars

7   Machine Learning Riddles and AI Self-Driving Cars

8   Spurring Financial Literacy via AI Self-Driving Cars

9   GM Cruise Minivan and AI Self-Driving Cars

10   Car Off Cliff Lessons and AI Self-Driving Cars

11 Daughter Prank and AI Self-Driving Cars

Advances in AI and Autonomous Vehicles: Cybernetic Self-Driving Cars

Practical Advances in Artificial Intelligence (AI) and Machine Learning

by

Dr. Lance B. Eliot, MBA, PhD

This title is available via Amazon and other book sellers

Companion Book By This Author

Self-Driving Cars:
"The Mother of All AI Projects"

by Dr. Lance B. Eliot, MBA, PhD

This title is available via Amazon and other book sellers

This title is available via Amazon and other book sellers

Lance B. Eliot

Companion Book By This Author

New Advances in AI Autonomous Driverless Cars Self-Driving Cars

by Dr. Lance B. Eliot, MBA, PhD

<u>Chapter Title</u>

1   Eliot Framework for AI Self-Driving Cars

2   Self-Driving Cars Learning from Self-Driving Cars

3   Imitation as Deep Learning for Self-Driving Cars

4   Assessing Federal Regulations for Self-Driving Cars

5   Bandwagon Effect for Self-Driving Cars

6   AI Backdoor Security Holes for Self-Driving Cars

7   Debiasing of AI for Self-Driving Cars

8   Algorithmic Transparency for Self-Driving Cars

9   Motorcycle Disentanglement for Self-Driving Cars

10 Graceful Degradation Handling of Self-Driving Cars

11 AI for Home Garage Parking of Self-Driving Cars

12 Motivational AI Irrationality for Self-Driving Cars

13 Curiosity as Cognition for Self-Driving Cars

14 Automotive Recalls of Self-Driving Cars

15 Internationalizing AI for Self-Driving Cars

16 Sleeping as AI Mechanism for Self-Driving Cars

17 Car Insurance Scams and Self-Driving Cars

18 U-Turn Traversal AI for Self-Driving Cars

19 Software Neglect for Self-Driving Cars

This title is available via Amazon and other book sellers

Companion Book By This Author
Introduction to
Driverless Self-Driving Cars
by Dr. Lance B. Eliot, MBA, PhD

Chapter Title

This title is available via Amazon and other book sellers

Companion Book By This Author

Autonomous Vehicle Driverless
Self-Driving Cars and Artificial Intelligence

by Dr. Lance B. Eliot, MBA, PhD

This title is available via Amazon and other book sellers

Companion Book By This Author

Transformative Artificial Intelligence Driverless Self-Driving Cars

by Dr. Lance B. Eliot, MBA, PhD

Chapter Title

This title is available via Amazon and other book sellers

Companion Book By This Author

**Disruptive Artificial Intelligence
and Driverless Self-Driving Cars**

by Dr. Lance B. Eliot, MBA, PhD

This title is available via Amazon and other book sellers

Companion Book By This Author

State-of-the-Art
AI Driverless Self-Driving Cars

by Dr. Lance B. Eliot, MBA, PhD

This title is available via Amazon and other book sellers

Lance B. Eliot

Companion Book By This Author

Top Trends in
AI Self-Driving Cars

by Dr. Lance B. Eliot, MBA, PhD

<u>Chapter Title</u>

This title is available via Amazon and other book sellers

Companion Book By This Author

***AI Innovations
and Self-Driving Cars***

by Dr. Lance B. Eliot, MBA, PhD

This title is available via Amazon and other book sellers

Companion Book By This Author

Crucial Advances for
AI Self-Driving Cars

by Dr. Lance B. Eliot, MBA, PhD

This title is available via Amazon and other book sellers

Companion Book By This Author

Sociotechnical Insights and
AI Driverless Cars

by Dr. Lance B. Eliot, MBA, PhD

This title is available via Amazon and other book sellers

Companion Book By This Author

Pioneering Advances for
AI Driverless Cars

by Dr. Lance B. Eliot, MBA, PhD

<u>Chapter Title</u>

This title is available via Amazon and other book sellers

Lance B. Eliot

Companion Book By This Author

Leading Edge Trends for
AI Driverless Cars

by Dr. Lance B. Eliot, MBA, PhD

This title is available via Amazon and other book sellers

The Cutting Edge of
AI Autonomous Cars

by Dr. Lance B. Eliot, MBA, PhD

Companion Book By This Author

The Next Wave of
AI Self-Driving Cars

by Dr. Lance B. Eliot, MBA, PhD

This title is available via Amazon and other book sellers

**Revolutionary Innovations of
AI Self-Driving Cars**

by Dr. Lance B. Eliot, MBA, PhD

This title is available via Amazon and other book sellers

Companion Book By This Author

AI Self-Driving Cars
Breakthroughs

by Dr. Lance B. Eliot, MBA, PhD

Chapter Title

This title is available via Amazon and other book sellers

Companion Book By This Author

Trailblazing Trends for
AI Self-Driving Cars

by Dr. Lance B. Eliot, MBA, PhD

Chapter Title

This title is available via Amazon and other book sellers

Companion Book By This Author

Ingenious Strides for
AI Driverless Cars

by Dr. Lance B. Eliot, MBA, PhD

This title is available via Amazon and other book sellers

Lance B. Eliot

Companion Book By This Author

***AI Self-Driving Cars
Inventiveness***

by Dr. Lance B. Eliot, MBA, PhD

<u>Chapter Title</u>

This title is available via Amazon and other book sellers

Visionary Secrets of
AI Driverless Cars

by Dr. Lance B. Eliot, MBA, PhD

Chapter Title

This title is available via Amazon and other book sellers

Companion Book By This Author

Spearheading
AI Self-Driving Cars

by Dr. Lance B. Eliot, MBA, PhD

Chapter Title

This title is available via Amazon and other book sellers

Companion Book By This Author

Spurring
AI Self-Driving Cars

by Dr. Lance B. Eliot, MBA, PhD

This title is available via Amazon and other book sellers

Companion Book By This Author

Avant-Garde
AI Driverless Cars

by Dr. Lance B. Eliot, MBA, PhD

This title is available via Amazon and other book sellers

Companion Book By This Author

AI Self-Driving Cars Evolvement

by Dr. Lance B. Eliot, MBA, PhD

This title is available via Amazon and other book sellers

Companion Book By This Author

AI Driverless Cars
Chrysalis
by Dr. Lance B. Eliot, MBA, PhD

This title is available via Amazon and other book sellers

Companion Book By This Author

Boosting
AI Autonomous Cars

by Dr. Lance B. Eliot, MBA, PhD

This title is available via Amazon and other book sellers

Companion Book By This Author

AI Self-Driving Cars Trendsetting

by Dr. Lance B. Eliot, MBA, PhD

This title is available via Amazon and other book sellers

Companion Book By This Author

AI Autonomous Cars
Forefront

by Dr. Lance B. Eliot, MBA, PhD

This title is available via Amazon and other book sellers

Companion Book By This Author

AI Autonomous Cars Emergence

by Dr. Lance B. Eliot, MBA, PhD

This title is available via Amazon and other book sellers

Companion Book By This Author

AI Autonomous Cars Progress

by Dr. Lance B. Eliot, MBA, PhD

This title is available via Amazon and other book sellers

<u>Companion Book By This Author</u>

AI Self-Driving Cars
Prognosis

by Dr. Lance B. Eliot, MBA, PhD

<u>Chapter Title</u>

This title is available via Amazon and other book sellers

Companion Book By This Author

AI Self-Driving Cars
Momentum

by Dr. Lance B. Eliot, MBA, PhD

This title is available via Amazon and other book sellers

Companion Book By This Author

AI Self-Driving Cars
Headway

by Dr. Lance B. Eliot, MBA, PhD

Chapter Title

This title is available via Amazon and other book sellers

Companion Book By This Author

AI Self-Driving Cars
Vicissitude

by Dr. Lance B. Eliot, MBA, PhD

This title is available via Amazon and other book sellers

Companion Book By This Author

AI Self-Driving Cars
Autonomy

by Dr. Lance B. Eliot, MBA, PhD

This title is available via Amazon and other book sellers

Companion Book By This Author

AI Driverless Cars Transmutation

by Dr. Lance B. Eliot, MBA, PhD

This title is available via Amazon and other book sellers

ABOUT THE AUTHOR

Dr. Lance B. Eliot, MBA, PhD is the CEO of Techbruim, Inc. and Executive Director of the Cybernetic AI Self-Driving Car Institute and has over twenty years of industry experience including serving as a corporate officer in a billion dollar firm and was a partner in a major executive services firm. He is also a serial entrepreneur having founded, ran, and sold several high-tech related businesses. He previously hosted the popular radio show *Technotrends* that was also available on American Airlines flights via their in-flight audio program. Author or co-author of a dozen books and over 400 articles, he has made appearances on CNN, and has been a frequent speaker at industry conferences.

A former professor at the University of Southern California (USC), he founded and led an innovative research lab on Artificial Intelligence in Business. Known as the "AI Insider" his writings on AI advances and trends has been widely read and cited. He also previously served on the faculty of the University of California Los Angeles (UCLA), and was a visiting professor at other major universities. He was elected to the International Board of the Society for Information Management (SIM), a prestigious association of over 3,000 high-tech executives worldwide.

He has performed extensive community service, including serving as Senior Science Adviser to the Vice Chair of the Congressional Committee on Science & Technology. He has served on the Board of the OC Science & Engineering Fair (OCSEF), where he is also has been a Grand Sweepstakes judge, and likewise served as a judge for the Intel International SEF (ISEF). He served as the Vice Chair of the Association for Computing Machinery (ACM) Chapter, a prestigious association of computer scientists. Dr. Eliot has been a shark tank judge for the USC Mark Stevens Center for Innovation on start-up pitch competitions, and served as a mentor for several incubators and accelerators in Silicon Valley and Silicon Beach. He served on several Boards and Committees at USC, including having served on the Marshall Alumni Association (MAA) Board in Southern California.

Dr. Eliot holds a PhD from USC, MBA, and Bachelor's in Computer Science, and earned the CDP, CCP, CSP, CDE, and CISA certifications. Born and raised in Southern California, and having traveled and lived internationally, he enjoys scuba diving, surfing, and sailing.

ADDENDUM

AI Driverless Cars Transmutation

*Practical Advances in Artificial Intelligence (AI)
and Machine Learning*

By
Dr. Lance B. Eliot, MBA, PhD

———

For supplemental materials of this book, visit:

www.ai-selfdriving-cars.guru

For special orders of this book, contact:

LBE Press Publishing

Email: LBE.Press.Publishing@gmail.com

www.ingramcontent.com/pod-product-compliance
Lightning Source LLC
Chambersburg PA
CBHW051046050326
40690CB00006B/622